T·L·C
FOR
AGING
PARENTS

T·L·C
FOR
AGING
PARENTS

A PRACTICAL GUIDE

BETTY BENSON ROBERTSON

Beacon Hill Press of Kansas City
Kansas City, Missouri

Copyright 1992
by Betty B. Robertson

ISBN: 083-411-4569
Printed in the
United States of America

Cover Design: Crandall Vail

10   9   8   7   6   5   4   3   2   1

In
loving memory
of
my father
Dr. Erwin G. Benson
1905-89
and
my mother
Elizabeth L. Benson
1909-91

I miss you both.
Thanks for everything!

DISCLAIMER

TLC for Aging Parents is not intended to serve as legal or medical advice or to endorse any product or service. It is meant to be an information resource and guide, and not a substitute for professional assistance.

If you are confused by anything you read in this book, or if you need more information, check with an expert. Of necessity, neither the author nor publisher of this book makes any guarantees regarding the outcome of the uses of this material. The ultimate responsibility for making good decisions is yours.

CONTENTS

		Page
Credits		**9**
Acknowledgments		**9**
Foreword		**11**

1: Pertaining to Preparation **13**
Ready or Not, Here It Comes / Searching the Scriptures /
The Aging Process / Role Reversal

2: Choosing to Care **19**
Biblical Norms / The Challenge / Caregivers Share

3: Rebuilding of Relationships **28**
Survey the Damage / Acknowledge the Pain from the Damage /
Write to Release the Feelings / List Personal Rights That Were
Violated / Yield Those Rights to God / List the Wrongs You Have
Done to Your Parents / Forgive / Seek Forgiveness / Desire
Reconciliation

4: Dealing with Decisions **33**
Steps / Guidelines

5: Overview of Options **37**
Independent Living / Semi-independent Living / Living with
Family / Nursing Home

6: Answers to Anxieties **46**
Legal Issues / Financial Matters

7: Observant to Organization **52**
Making Life Easier / Locating Help

8: Facing the Feelings **59**
Negative Collage / Proper Perspective / About This Thing
Called Love / Family Meetings

9: Challenge of Coping   63
    Daily Prayer / Daily Bible Reading / Scripture Memorization /
    Focus on Positive Aspects / Prayer Partner / Accepting Help /
    Daily Journal / Support Group / Laugh / Exercise / Working at
    Home / Sandwich Generation Resources

10: Dealing with Death   70
    Being Realistic / Planning Ahead / Requested Measures of Care /
    How to Recognize Death / Steps to Take / Facing Death in the
    Hospital / Facing Death at Home / Hospice / When It's Time
    to Say Good-bye / Daddies Don't Die / Letting Go / What Now? /
    Closure / Give Yourself Time / Life Goes On

Afterword   78

Appendix   79
    Daily Care Plan / Funeral Planning Form / Health Insurance
    Record / Home Safety Checklist / Medical History Chart /
    Medicine Chart / Monthly Meal Planner / Nursing Home
    Checklist / "One Anothers" of Scripture / Prayer Requests

Bibliography   103

CREDITS

"Caring for Our Aging Parents," by Bonnie Jamison. Originally appeared in *Alliance Life*. Used by permission.

"God Is in Control," by Sherri Langton. Used by permission.

"Changing Places," used by permission from Bud Atkinson.

"Praying Is Easy," by Millie Deitz. Originally appeared in *Standard*, Beacon Hill Press of Kansas City. Used by permission.

"Character Qualities." From *Advanced Leadership Guide*. Copyright 1978 by Institute in Basic Youth Conflicts. Reproduced by permission of the Institute in Basic Life Principles.

Some of the concepts in Chapter 3 were adapted from materials presented by the Institute in Basic Life Principles. Used by permisson.

"Full Circle," by Marilyn Hamilton. Used by permission.

ACKNOWLEDGMENTS

My special thanks to:

- Earl, my husband, for his loving support, invaluable insights, and unflagging confidence

- Shawn and Sherri, our children, for willingly enduring the adjustments involved in generations living together and for cheerfully helping

- Deborah Jarmul, whose professional comments and perceptive advice added to the preparation of this book

- K. C. Mason for the long, tedious hours spent copyediting

- Jan Obar for properly mixing criticism with encouragement and offering excellent editorial assistance

- Joan Kilpatrick, Marie Lowry, Lois Rigel, and Dee Vandergrift, prayer partners

- Betty Avis, D. Martin Butler, Kathy Butts, Diane Carnell, Melba Case, Cathie Davis, Iris Edwards, Phyllis Folsom, Bonnie Jamison, Andrea North, Linnea Oke, Shirley Posey, Pat Rulo, Joseph Starmann, and Margaret Whitlatch for their contributions

- Marilyn Ferrario, Arlene Sandler, and Sandra Stewart-Cole, librarians at Kingshighway Branch Library, St. Louis, for their splendid cooperation

FOREWORD

You made a wise choice—you opened the book! You are holding a collection of accounts involving love and hard work. This is a compilation of emotions and experiences induced by love.

Love. What an amazing four-letter word! It can produce a barrage of responses. One response to love is care giving. Caring for the older adult is an issue dear to me as a gerontologist and to the author of this book.

What does Betty Robertson know of caring for an older adult? A few years ago the answer would have been, not much. Since then, Betty, with the support of family and friends, has cared for her parents in her home. She has learned a great deal about the older adult, as well as herself, the adult child.

The adult child. A complex title. With it, we are expected to respond as adults, yet remember who is the parent. Keep this concept in your heart and mind. When you become the caregiver, it is easy to lose track of role definitions. Betty has given excellent examples within these pages related to role reversals and the dangers associated with the misuse of this phenomenon.

This role of care giving can be confrontation with love. Betty has learned the art of loving encounters. Care giving often means facing issues head-on. She has also learned, and teaches through this book, another very important point. Issues are one thing, parents are another.

Within this book, you will find practical ideas and beneficial resources. Betty discusses the feelings of resentment, anger, grief, pain, and satisfaction. How can a person deal with these feelings if one has not had any experience with them? She has and now shares beautifully in *TLC for Aging Parents.*

Read on, please. The professional side of this gerontologist pensively applauds your willingness to endure hardships while caring for your special older adult with love and dignity. My adult child side certainly understands why you have chosen to do so.

God's blessing on you and the older adult for whom you are caring. God's blessing on Betty Robertson, my courageous author-friend, for tearing down old walls and building great new paths for others.

Deborah B. Jarmul, *President*
HEALTH CARE CONCEPTS
St. Louis

ONE

Pertaining to Preparation

A wise man thinks ahead.   PROV. 13:16, TLB

The friend on the phone was saying, "I know you and your brothers are scattered across the country, but someone needs to come home. Your father is so weak, he cannot care for himself. Your mother has been regressing mentally and no longer can make decisions or adequately care for your father."

After careful deliberation and intense prayer, a decision was formed and arrangements made to move my parents in with our family. At that moment, I willingly enlisted. I was now a member of the "Sandwich Generation"—an army of people caring for both children and parents. Nothing in the basic training of life prepared me for what was ahead as a caregiver and health-care provider.

Until then, words such as *ostomy, Foley catheter, duodenum dressing, decubitus ulcer, dementia,* and *incontinence* were irrelevant entries in Webster's dictionary. Soon after, definitions erupted into reality.

Until then, things such as bathtub safety rails, transfer bench, deluxe portable commode, folding walker, flotation cushion, Depend shields, safety vest, and ostomy pouches were products in a medical catalog. Now they all occupied my home.

Until then, I was free to set my own schedule. Now my entire life revolved around pill schedules, bathroom needs, doctors' appointments, and the myriad of concerns involved in caring for aging parents.

Some days I felt like I was in a combat zone, dodging the bullets of change. When the fears, frustrations, and fatigue overwhelmed, I dug a denial trench to escape the complex issues.

How was I going to handle caring for aging parents? Until then, I was the "baby girl." Suddenly the roles reversed. I was tucking my parents in bed and telling them to sleep tight. I was arranging doctor's appointments and dispensing medications. I was helping dress, bathe, and groom my parents. The adjustment to this emotional upheaval was taxing.

Ready or Not, Here It Comes

Ready or not, I was suddenly confronted with caring for my aging parents. This is happening all around the country, for the American population is getting older. The National Institute of Aging reports, "The fastest-growing population segment is composed of individuals over the age of 80."

The U.S. Census Bureau estimates that the over-85 age-group will grow from 3 million to 8.6 million by the year 2020 and to 17.8 million by 2040 (*Health Update*, April 1991). These statistics indicate that a growing segment of our society could become involved in caring for elderly parents.

People are living longer because of momentous advances in medical technology. Medicines have eliminated many diseases. Concentrated public health awareness and education have resulted in better health and longevity. In the meantime, birthrates are dropping. Ken Dychtwald says, "These features are coming together to create a massive demographic shift" (*Age Wave* [Los Angeles: Jeremy P. Tarcher, 1989]).

Those who are still healthy, energetic, independent, and mentally alert might be called the "young old." The "old old," on the other hand, show evidence of declining vitality, physical strength, and sometimes mental acuity. Six million elderly Americans need help getting out of bed and using the bathroom. Millions more can't manage meals, money, or transportation.

Caring for aging parents is a major issue. Seven million family members spend part of their day caring for an aged parent. This care is either in their own homes or doing essential errands and chores. Many women spend more years caring for their dependent parents than for their children. The Older Women's League (OWL) estimates American women will spend 17 years raising children and 18 years helping aged parents.

As American society awakens to an aging population's needs, providing care for parents becomes a new developmental stage in life. Often adult children have no training or information on geriatric problems, or even a frame of reference from which to operate.

Dianne and J. T., for example, are both in their mid-30s. They have been married 10 years and parent three young children. Both had child rearing training, but nothing in their life experiences prepared them for taking care of J. T.'s 70-year-old mother. As Dianne related, "We are moving my mother-in-law to live with us. I can't imagine the adjustments this will mean. I don't know anything about caring for an older adult."

Preparation is seldom made for the eventuality of old age, even though it happens to most people. Many don't prepare because they fear becoming older or don't know how. The prevalent philosophy is: "I'll do whatever is necessary when the time comes"—hoping, of course, the time never comes!

Adult children try to avoid the issue. They think, My parents will never get old; they will never get sick; nothing will ever change. But all parents are going to age. Every adult needs to face the possibility of becoming their parents' teacher, monitor, and caregiver. By facing that reality and learning how to act and react, the unknown future can be bearable.

Searching the Scriptures

Preparation for parent care begins with an understanding of Scripture. Deut. 5:16 says, *Honor your father and your mother, as the Lord your God has commanded you, so that you may live long and that it may go well with you in the land the Lord your God is giving you.* This mandate occurs in a slightly different form in Lev. 19:3: *Each of you must respect his mother and father.*

Commentators agree on this commandment's original intent. Adult children are to honor their aged parents with reverence, care, and support. The practical application is a personal matter and varies in each situation, but the directive remains.

Until the middle of the 20th century, family circles were compact geographically and closer emotionally. Tradition authorized grandparents living with families of the next two generations until they died. Children benefited from the extra love and wisdom afforded by the different generation surrounding them.

Following the baby boom of World War II, the situation changed. Families became increasingly mobile because of jobs, divorce, and moving to the suburbs. This geographical dispersion hindered families from staying in touch. Emphasis turned from extended family to nuclear family, from stability to mobility, from focusing on what parents did right to what they did all wrong.

Regardless of new family configurations, the basic principle remains: adult children are to honor their parents. Walter Harrelson suggests: "It is how one deals with those who can no longer fend for themselves, and with such helpless ones against whom one has a lifetime of grievances for wrongs done or imagined, that provides the test of one's moral and human commitments" (*The Ten Commandments and Human Rights* [Philadelphia: Fortress Press, 1980]).

We honor our fathers and mothers because we have received so much from them, including life itself. We owe our parents for all the benefits they offered us in our early development. Our gratitude often is mixed with resentment about their perceived shortcomings and imperfections. This is not an appropriate time to dump old conflicts on aging parents. Release the past through forgiveness. This is discussed in chapter 3. Making peace is crucial before involving yourself in parent care.

Honoring your parents has nothing to do with whether or not you like them. It means, rather, not shaming them verbally or minimizing the investment they have made in our lives.

- Is derogatory speaking honoring?
- Is unkind treatment honoring?
- Is rejecting honoring?
- Is recalling past shortcomings honoring?
- Is acting only in our best interests honoring?
- Is neglecting honoring?

It is the adult child's stated responsibility to care for elderly parents, even at the sacrifice of time, resources, and emotional energy. While each situation is unique and no specific rules can be established, the commandment to esteem remains.

Jesus stressed the fifth commandment's absolute nature. He criticized the Pharisees, who abused the religious vows to escape caring for their parents. Jesus labeled as hypocrites those who would deny support for their parents because what was intended for the parents was given to God (Matt. 15:1-9; Mark 7:9-13).

First Tim. 5:8 says: *If anyone does not provide for his relatives, and especially for his immediate family, he has denied the faith and is worse than an unbeliever.* This includes both financial and emotional support. It goes beyond sending checks, or finding adequate housing for elderly parents, to making time—perhaps the greatest need of all.

Why honor father and mother? Because God commands it. His directives are never without foundation in reason and systematic order. His established order is that the present adult generation honors the previous; the children honor the adult. When God's command is obeyed, the sequence is established, and the positive progression continues from generation to generation. Children will learn by following their parents' example. They will learn to respect their parents when they observe their grandparents being held in high esteem.

The Aging Process

Parent care preparation continues by an understanding of the aging process. Limitations in old age are to be expected. The Bible describes individuals who suffered infirmities common to aging: Isaac and Jacob were blind in old age (Gen. 27:1-2; 48:10); and Eli was overweight and blind (1 Sam. 4:12-18).

Scripture also has examples of people who grew old well. At 85 years of age Caleb said, *I am as strong this day as I was in the day that Moses sent me* (Josh. 14:10-11, KJV). When Moses was 120, *His eye was not dim, nor his natural force abated* (Deut. 34:7, KJV).

A biblical view of the elderly promotes understanding and preparation for possible parent care:

- Infirmities often come with aging (Eccles. 12:1-7).
- Old age can be characterized by beauty (Prov. 16:31; 20:29).
- Some older adults are revealed as good and wise (Isaac, Gen. 35:28-29; Joseph, 50:22)
- Other elderly people are described as foolish (Eccles. 4:13; Eli, who was a morally weak 98-year-old)

Aging effects cannot be predicted. In biblical times, as today, most people carried their personality traits with them into old age. But tragically some illnesses change personalities.

Become educated on your parents' specific infirmities. An examination by a qualified physician can assess their condition. Ask questions and understand the prognosis. Ample material is available at public libraries on common illnesses of the older adult.

Role Reversal

A final step in preparing for the eventuality of caring for aging parents involves examining how you feel about the possibility of becoming your parents' "parent." Role reversal is one of the hardest aspects of parent care.

As I was helping Daddy into bed one night, he said, "You begin life with your mother tucking you in. You end it with your daughter doing it!" We laughed, but our hearts wept.

Do you remember helping your 2-year-old child pull up his underwear after going potty? Yes, but have you helped your 83-year-old father retrieve his boxers because he was too weak to do it himself? It's different. You think, Why does this hurt so much? Because, inside, I'm still his little girl.

The sudden, or growing, helplessness of people who were authority figures in a child's life can be overwhelming. This causes sorrow and a deep sense of loss as the mighty figures of childhood become needy and vulnerable.

When parents age and begin to confront new problems, adult children find the roles reversing. Parents seem like children—dependent, sometimes demanding, possibly needing more than can be given. The mother and father who nurtured, comforted, and provided shelter are growing old. Now they need the watchful tenderness that is the birthright of every child. It is now our responsibility to care for aging parents. This change of roles is extremely difficult.

The one constant in life is change. Although not always noticeable, change is inevitable in every life period. It is an inescapable fact of life. To live is to change. Scripture reminds us: *There is a time for everything, and a season for every activity under heaven* (Eccles. 3:1).

Resisting change is normal, but eventually it must be confronted. There are two choices: openly cope and decide upon a response, or be dragged through change in spite of yourself! Bud Atkinson, in his poem "Changing Places," expresses his inner feelings about role reversal:

> *Yes, he's a little older now,*
> *The once proud head begins to bow;*
> *The man who was strong and bold,*
> *We must admit, is growing old.*
>
> *The puzzled look upon his face*
> *That says I've taken Daddy's place;*
> *It's hard for him to understand,*
> *Now he's the child, and I'm the man.*
>
> *The dad who used to lead the way,*
> *Who guarded us both night and day,*
> *Now gives to me his trembling hand.*
> *He's the child, and I'm the man.*

The inner feelings of parents placed in this role reversal are often hard for them to understand, let alone talk about, but it is an essential part of the preparation process.

Understand what your parents desire. Quality of life means different things to the adult child than it does to the parent. The child worries about the parent's security. The parent is concerned about maintaining control of life. Be sensitive to underlying fears.

Adult children sometimes disregard a parent's method of doing things. They try to impose their own agenda instead. Your parents don't need a barrage of nonstop advice. Unless the counsel given is essential to their safety, offer it and leave it!

Make decisions with them, not for them. Grasp the partnership concept. Even when adult children need to make a decision for their parents, involve them in it.

We already have experienced being our parents' children. We also understand what it means to be our children's parents. But becoming our parents' "parent" is entirely new. This responsibility need not be so overwhelming and the details so endless if time is taken to discern our parents' needs, problems, feelings, and capabilities.

Learning about the older adult and putting that knowledge in practice are two separate issues. Even with excellent understanding of older adults in general, an effort must be made to learn about parents' hopes for the future. Evaluate their needs by talking with them.

In response to the question, "What do you think about growing old?" my father answered, "It's for the birds." He laughed, but tears were in his eyes.

"It's hard to express what I feel," Mother said. "I never thought we'd have to live with our children like this. But we're glad we can spend the rest of our lives with you."

My elderly aunt commented, "I would rather die first than inflict myself on my kids."

Everyone wants to be independent. But hearty minds and spry bodies do not always accompany old age. The most frequent fear of aging people is the deterioration of their health.

The cornerstone to helping everyone through the role reversal process is learning how to discuss sensitive and difficult topics. Dr. Richard Johnson says, "You can focus primarily on the content of what is being said, or you can expand your focus to include the feelings behind the statements." In his book, *Aging Parents—How to Understand and Help Them* (Liguori, Mo.: Liguori Publications), Dr. Johnson explains a five-step procedure to enhance communication with aging parents.

Another beneficial resource to help you become your parents' "parent" is Mark A. Edinberg's book, *Talking with Your Aging Parents* (New York: Shambhala Publications, 1987). The author offers practical skills, strategies, and support to the adult child for discussing important issues.

❖ ❖ ❖

DISCUSSION QUESTIONS

1. The Bible says to honor and respect your father and mother. What does "honor" and "respect" mean?
2. How can you prepare for care giving?
3. What does old age mean to you?
4. When did you first notice your parents were aging? How did you feel?
5. How do you feel about the possibility of becoming your parents' "parent"?
6. What fears do you think your parents may have?
7. What fears do you have about your parents aging?
8. What does Isa. 46:3-4 mean to you?
9. Why is communication between adult child and aging parent so important?

———— TWO ————

Choosing to Care

God is able to make all grace abound to you, so that in all things at all times, having all that you need, you will abound in every good work.   2 COR. 9:8

Biblical Norms

The Bible presents standards for measuring acts and attitudes toward aging parents:

- *Do not despise your mother when she is old* (Prov. 23:22).
- *Rise in the presence of the aged, show respect for the elderly and revere your God* (Lev. 19:32).
- *Whoever wants to become great among you must be your servant . . . For even the Son of Man did not come to be served, but to serve, and to give his life as a ransom for many* (Mark 10:43, 45).
- *Let us stop just <u>saying</u> we love people; let us <u>really</u> love them, and <u>show</u> <u>it</u> by our <u>actions</u>* (1 John 3:18, TLB, underlines in text).

In our society, adult children and their parents may live distances apart. This poses special difficulties, but the principle remains. God wants to help aging parents through their children. The "really shoulds" of today will become the "if onlys" of tomorrow if action is not taken.

The Challenge

Love is the heart quality that makes it possible to meet the care-giving challenge. The shape love takes is determined by each individual situation. Choosing to care is a beginning. The outcome depends upon these factors:

- Are the aging parents active, healthy, and on the go?
- Are the older adults living on their own, with a modified life-style due to illness?
- Are the elderly individuals unable to function on their own?

We are to love all persons, with a love lived out in action. In daily living, this may mean using limited resources in providing for aging parents. It may mean giving practical help where needed. Jarvik and Small report, "One-fourth of all individuals who live beyond 85 need help in walking; one in 10 needs help in dressing and toileting; one in 20 hardly ever gets out of bed; and one in 25 has to be fed by someone else" (*Parentcare* [New York: Crown Publishers, 1988]).

Caring will mean sacrifices in one's present life. When engrossed in caring, the caregiver senses a deep sense of satisfaction surfacing. The majority of women on the "daughter track" do not want to give up their family responsibilities—no matter what personal or professional sacrifices it entails. They see their efforts as a chance to repay the time and care their parents gave them—an opportunity to say again, "I love you," before it's too late. Tracy Green and Todd Temple suggest, "Whether your parents are living at home or in a nursing home, across town or across the country, whether they're sugary sweet or just plain impossible—you can make a difference in their lives" (*52 Ways to Show Aging Parents You Care* [Nashville: Thomas Nelson Publishers, 1992]).

Caregivers Share

What she speaks cannot be understood. She does not often comprehend what I am saying to her. Others must help with all her personal needs. She does not eat but drinks a special formula from a cup. She does not walk.

This description fits two individuals I chose to care for. One was our three-month-old daughter. The other was my 82-year-old mother! Our infant daughter represented limitless potential. My mother, because of multiple physical and mental problems, represented encroaching death. Still, I chose to care.

Tied by soft chains of love and blood, many others have elected to attend their aging parents. Some of their testimonies follow.

Betty Avis

My mother broke her pelvis and was unable to care for herself. Her mind also began to deteriorate. At first, my two sisters and I brought her into our three homes on a rotation basis. This was difficult for all and soon became confusing to Mother.

We began the search for a nursing home. The good ones were filled. The others looked and smelled so poorly, we decided against them.

Eventually a group home was decided upon. A private party housed six elderly people. Every time I picked up Mom for a visit and took her back, I felt sick inside. After nine months, I felt she was not getting the care and attention she needed. This is when God spoke to my husband and me about taking her into our home.

At that time, I had been with the school district for nearly 10 years. It was a job with continual opportunities for advancement. When the thought first crossed my mind to quit work and take Mother out of the nursing home, I pushed it away, thinking, There is no way we can handle the financial demands.

But Gary and I prayed about it. Soon we knew for certain this was God's plan, at this time, for our lives. We learned God supplies all needs.

I quit my job, and Mother came to live with us. I take her with me everywhere. I load up the wheelchair, and off we go! Each week we go to a local department store to shop and have an inexpensive lunch. Due to Mother's dementia some things she says are embarrassing. I just smile —and thank God for the sense of humor He gave me!

Rom. 5:3-4 (KJV) says, *We glory in tribulations also: knowing that tribulation worketh patience; and patience, experience; and experience, hope.* I'm not sure about the *glory* part! I don't feel a great deal yet—but I have never regretted the decision to move Mother into our home. During these four years of care giving, God has developed character qualities in me. I rejoice in the changes He continues to make in my life.

I feel my story has just begun. Mom is now suffering from dementia, and we are really being stretched. I don't know the future, but I know God holds my hand.

A favorite verse of mine is, *But the mercy of the Lord is from everlasting to everlasting upon them that fear him, and his righteousness unto children's children* (Ps. 103:17, KJV).

Kathy Butts

I was a single career woman, working at our denominational headquarters. Because of my job, I had the privilege of meeting Dr. T. W. Willingham. Shortly after meeting him, I was visiting in their home. I met his 85-year-old wife, who was a semi-invalid. I noticed she needed help with daily living activities.

One day, I had a direct assignment from the Lord. His message to me was: "I want you to minister to the Willinghams!" There was no supporting scripture at that time, but across the years, that directive sustained me, strengthened me, and kept me going. Numerous verses were used of the Lord during the next 22 years of caring for the Willinghams.

Sitting at the feet of Dr. T. W. Willingham on a daily basis, picking his heart and brain, researching Scripture for his writings, typing manuscripts, editing tapes—all of these were bonuses to the cooking, cleaning, laundry, and personal care for Mrs. Willingham.

My decision to adopt a set of older adults actually gave me life. It was like a transformation and a transfusion through my veins.

If you talked to my boss of those years, he would tell you I became a better employee. At no time did my caring project interfere with my office work.

How did I cope? With tears and TOTAL DEPENDENCE on the ONE who called me to the task. First Thess. 5:24 (KJV) says: *Faithful is he that calleth you, who also will do it.* God will not ask us to do anything that HE will not enable us to do!

When I look back at my schedule during those years, I know the Lord's miraculous power kept me going. I came to work on time and went to the Willingham home during my lunch hour to prepare their meal. Right after work, I fixed supper. Then we worked a couple of hours on research, typing, or editing. This was my schedule five days a week. When Dr. T. W. was away preaching, I moved in with Mrs. Willingham for two to three weeks. I would get her up, fed, and fixed for the morning. I read many books to her during those evening hours.

My caring involved giving up my own plans. I was dating a young man when the Lord gave me my directive. He was a wonderful Christian, just what I had dreamed. I knew I could not marry him, even though he was sure, and still fulfill my assignment. I will always remember the night I tearfully told him good-bye. But, oh, how the Lord made it up to me.

Did I learn anything that might help other caregivers? *Whatever He says to you, DO IT!* (John 2:5, NASB, emphasis added). If God should choose you to care for older adults, He will enable. It will take a willingness to be completely guided by Him. Older adults are full of lessons, humor, and experiences that enrich our lives.

This was indeed the case: *Thou art come to the kingdom for such a time as this* (Esther 4:14*b*, KJV).

Melba Case

My husband and I are caring for both our mothers and an aunt. One mother, age 79, lives in a church-owned retirement center and requires assistance with her daily living. We buy groceries, shop, pay bills, do laundry, and prepare medications so that they will be taken correctly. The other mother, age 85, and aunt, age 82, are sisters and live alone in their own homes. They have serious health problems but are very independent. We assist them with home and car repairs, health insurance forms, and business affairs when requested. It is our hope to offer enough support so that they can remain independent as long as possible.

We love our family and want them to be well cared for, but having sole responsibility really wears one down. We both plan to retire soon. We have raised and educated three children. We love to travel and would like to develop some hobbies. Yet, almost all our free time is spent as caregivers. Our greatest need is for some short-time relief.

We are now participating in a support group of children with aging parents. This has been the best thing to happen to us. There have been special speakers. We support each other, share ideas, and are developing a sense of humor about our problems.

Two Scripture verses have helped us: *In the same way, the Spirit helps us in our weakness. We do not know what we ought to pray for, but the Spirit himself intercedes for us with groans that words cannot express* (Rom. 8:26); and *I know what it is to be in need, and I know what it is to have plenty. I have learned the secret of being content in any and every situation, whether well fed or hungry, whether living in plenty or in want. I can do everything through him who gives me strength* (Phil. 4:12-13).

Iris Edwards

I am 76 but sometimes feel double that! My mother is 99 years old. She has been with us off and on for the last 5 years. Originally, she was recovering from two broken hips. She stayed the night with us, eating dinner and breakfast, but went home for the day. We lived next door to each other. Recently, she had some trouble and has been with us since.

I couldn't do this without my husband's help. My brother comes by every couple of weeks to take her to the doctor.

It would be nice to have a few days away, but she doesn't want anyone else doing for her. So I have made up my mind to keep going as long as I can, or as long as is necessary. I certainly have learned patience through all of this.

Phyllis Folsom

Since I am the only girl and have always been close to both Mom and Dad, it's always been agreed I would care for my folks when needed. Daddy died a few years ago. When we moved to Durango and designed our house, we did it with Mother in mind. The bottom floor is self-contained, with an outside entrance. Doorways are wide enough for a wheelchair, if that were ever needed.

Right after Mom's 70th birthday, she announced, "I am putting my home up for sale and moving to Durango." The upkeep on her house and yard was getting to be too much. Her widow friends were beginning to move away to be with their kids.

She did not want to live with us yet. We found a two-year-old mobile home with a beautiful view. It is on the way to town and church.

I'm thankful this situation has worked out so well. At first, I was really scared. I feel the next step will be easier to face since we've had this time to get to know each other and build bonds. Each set of circumstances creates its own problems and emotions. Time is needed to sort them out and commit them to God.

Bonnie Jamison

When the doctors told me that my mother, the victim of Lou Gehrig's disease (amyotrophic lateral sclerosis), had only a few weeks to live, I knew I had to make a decision. Would I leave her in the nursing home, or would I take her home and care for her during the last weeks of her life?

I decided I could be inconvenienced for a few weeks. After all, I reasoned, Mother had given me years of her life.

But as my family and I were soon to find out, the decision to bring my mother home made an enormous difference in our lives.

Naturally, I became anxious thinking about the demands and responsibility her care would put on my family. Her physical abilities were limited to blinking her eyes, moaning, and swallowing pureed food. I was overwhelmed at the thought of meeting her total physical and emotional needs 24 hours a day, even for a few weeks.

Mother's care was a challenge, but my family and I never thought of it as a burden. Burdens are for people who never have tasted the thrill of having personal and meaningful relationships with a dying person and a living God.

Our family determined to become Mother's support team, playing vital roles in her life. We became partners with each other and with God. Our deepening bonds shattered many obstacles, and Mother's care grew to be a part of our lives.

Not one of us was qualified to fulfill the myriad of responsibilities, but God provided our strength, *For when I am weak, then I am strong* (2 Cor. 12:10). Though at times the challenges were painful, they never were regrettable.

The situations I had dreaded most became times of great character growth in each of our lives. I had been reluctant for my young teenagers, ages 11 through 16, to see and help with Mother's most basic physical needs. I wanted to shield them and preserve their fond memories of a loving, healthy grandmother.

One night when Mother accidentally wet the bed, I reacted in frustration. I threw myself on my bed, crying, "I can't take this anymore!" Once my tears subsided, I headed toward Mother's room, only to hear my children laughing and talking. They had sensed my despair and had taken control of the situation—bathing Mother, changing the sheets, and lifting her spirits with love and laughter.

Our children contributed enormously to Mother's happiness. The experience of having her in our home had positive effects on their lives as they exhibited unselfish attitudes, loyalty, and love toward their grandmother.

Friends and hired help became important figures in our daily routine as well, as they provided much-needed freedom for us.

We watched Mother willfully surrender her life to Jesus and be content in His protective love. Her unquenchable desire to draw closer to Him was fascinating: she began a ministry of prayer for our family and those she loved. Her days continued to hold purpose.

The value of a life is incalculable. Fortunately for my family and me, we stopped long enough to hear the voice of one dying, and to hear God's voice as well. We received a priceless legacy. The predicted three weeks stretched into four incredible years. They were perhaps the most enriching years of our lives yet.

God gave us the privilege of caring for a fragile human being. The seemingly dreadful affliction gave birth to a profound and lasting faith for all of us and brought abundant blessings.

Does the word *provide* in 1 Tim. 5:8 necessarily mean bringing our parents into our homes? I do not believe so. There are alternatives that must be considered: remaining in their own environments with outside help as it becomes necessary; a retirement community; living with another relative or friend; or a residential care/nursing home facility. All of these should be discussed with elderly parents if at all possible. By "providing," I believe God means for us lovingly to meet their needs to the best of our abilities.

Facing a decision like this should become a matter of deep, committed prayer. Ask God for the wisdom He promises, then take time to search the Scriptures. Carefully investigate nursing facilities or other sources of outside help. By revealing His plan, God will allow you to grant an honorable "last wish" for your aging parents and will fill you with His unselfish love and infinite grace.

Kendra Morrison

I am a single professional, presently in business for myself. This gave me the freedom to follow the promptings of the Lord to move and tend to my 86-year-old uncle. I moved largely to take the burden off my brother, who was his only caregiver.

My family has a long history of taking care of older family members. It is a natural thing for me and my siblings to do. My aunt never married because she always was taking care of someone. I remember visiting her when I was very young. There were eight other people living in her house—all family members. I guess she became a role model for me at a very early age.

There have certainly been some adjustments on my part. My uncle will not take a bath or shower. He insists he's keeping clean with sink spit baths. The lack of underwear in his laundry, and his body odor, tell me he isn't.

He's extremely sloppy when he washes his face, shaves, and brushes his teeth. I have to clean the bathroom sink every day before I can use it. He tries to clean it up, but his eyesight is bad. The toilet is much the same.

I don't know where to get help for his personal hygiene and incontinence problem. My uncle is not open to talking about it. He is convinced going to the doctor will not do any good, and that all the medical community wants is his money.

He sent for a living will but, to my knowledge, has not yet signed it. I know he doesn't want any extraordinary means taken to prolong his life. He would be very happy just to die in his sleep at home. It's kind of funny. We've been able to talk more about his death than about his need to take a bath. I believe God's grace will be sufficient when I wake up one morning and he is gone. I really do hope it happens that way. But if there is a medical crisis and hospital decisions have to be made, I believe we are prepared to make them.

I have many conflicting emotions. I'm sad watching the gradual losses occurring. Sometimes I feel guilty that I am not doing enough; other times I feel manipulated into doing unnecessary things. Those are the times when the Lord speaks to my heart about having love and compassion.

Overall, my biggest burden is not having "my place" to live. I'm in someone else's home. I don't always feel I can do things my way.

I believe God has given me freedom from the burdens of a family of my own so that I can be a servant to others. If I am being obedient to a call for this form of ministry, God will give me the grace to accomplish it.

Andrea North

My mother is 81. She has arthritis, has a lung disease, and has lost sight in one eye. She lives in her own home, but I have been helping with the finances and household chores for two years.

The biggest problem I face is keeping myself from becoming consumed by my mother's life. There are not enough hours in the day to run her home and take care of mine also.

I believe I am a more caring person and have greater patience because of what I have been doing. It hasn't been easy, and I pray much that the Lord will guide me and help me be patient with my mother and others.

Linnea Oke

When we moved to Colorado Springs, I asked my folks to come live with us. Mother was having progressive arthritic problems. We built a duplex, and they lived on their side.

One and a half years later, Mother had a stroke. After some therapy, I was able to care for her in their side of the house, with help from my father and visiting nurses. She died with a heart attack.

Dad lived for 14 more years. He received no nursing care, just meals, laundry, and housecleaning. Two years before he died, he was in the hospital. I was having major surgery, and the doctor felt I could not care for him at home. So we had him placed in a nursing home in the city. I visited daily and took him for frequent car rides. He died at age 99.

I don't regret one day of the care, work, worry, stress, or time. I only wish I could have done more.

Rev. Joseph W. Starmann

Both my mother and father suffer from a variety of ailments. I felt it necessary to take a leave of absence from my job as priest. Caring for my aged parents at their home—and helping to preserve their dwindling financial resources—is a top priority for me.

I know my decision to interrupt my work this way is a bit unusual. By some family's standards, my parents would be prime candidates for a nursing home. But I oppose taking that step. I think it's important to keep them in comfortable, familiar surroundings as long as possible.

Margaret Whitlatch

I am the only child and have full responsibility, since my mother is unable to make decisions for herself. She lived in our home for two months. A day care was available for aging persons, just five blocks from our home. I would take her to this center one day a week. This enabled me to have a day away and provided a new interest for Mother. Although we got along well, our home was never "home" to her. Home, to her, was her apartment, where she had lived for the past 11 years. She was physically unable to be alone any longer.

Her condition deteriorated to the point that our physician advised me I was unable to care for her. She was placed in "swing bed" (intermediate care) in the local hospital. Her name was placed on the waiting list for an opening in the nursing home. Soon an opening developed, and she was transferred there. The nursing home is located in a wing of the local hospital.

The placement of Mother in a nursing home has been a traumatic experience for me. I have come to the conclusion that residence in the nursing home is for her best interest. They have the facilities, equipment, menu, and trained personnel for her comfort and well-being. The home is well managed with compassionate staff personnel and hygienic facilities.

I visit with my mother every afternoon from about 3:00 to 5:00. During this time we read her mail, look at family pictures, talk about the family, tidy up the room, and arrange her clothing. I sometimes wheel her to the coffee shop for coffee and pastry. On occasion, my husband will join us, and we arrange to have her meal tray delivered to the hospital dining room where we have our meal together. This gives her the feeling we have "gone out" for a meal.

There are times when I cry, but these times are tempered by the moments of laughter at some of the strange figments of her imagination. Maintaining a sense of humor, along with a compassionate heart, are essential when passing through this experience. Every time I visit I assure Mother of my love. When God chooses to take her home to heaven, I want to have no regrets for having failed to show proper care and love.

DISCUSSION QUESTIONS

1. What is God's grace and how does it relate to caring for aging parents?
2. What does Prov. 23:22 mean to you?
3. How do you _show_ . . . _by [y]our actions_ (1 John 3:18, TLB) that you really love your parents?
4. Which testimonial spoke to you and why?
5. Are you willing to commit to caring for your aging parents in whatever manner seems appropriate for your parents' individual needs?

God Is in Control
by Sherri Langton

When reality batters and breaks me,
My hope hugs the sidelines,
My faith loses pace;
When discouragement shatters and shakes me
And tempts me to quit,
To concede in the race—
I hold to this truth for trusting;
It fastens my eyes on the goal.
I've measured its length
And tested its strength:
God is in control!

T H R E E

Rebuilding of Relationships

Forgive as the Lord forgave you.   COL. 3:13

Beth, a Christian woman in her middle 40s, did not realize she harbored painful childhood memories and hidden resentments until her mother moved in with her. She then began showing symptoms of physical and emotional stress. Tension stemmed from unresolved conflicts with her mother. Beth had never believed she measured up to her mother's perfectionist standards. She resented her mother's strong arm of control. Hands-on, loving nurturing was uncommon.

Beth had concealed her animosity behind a protective wall. But with her mother living in her home, childhood incidents hidden in the recesses of memory surfaced.

Bricks of resentment, bitterness, and anger build emotional walls between parents and children. Past relationships govern present feelings. When the topic of caring for aging parents is broached, responses often are negative. If the following scriptural guidelines are followed, the walls will come tumbling down.

Jesus said, *If you forgive other people their failures, your Heavenly Father will also forgive you. But if you will not forgive . . . neither will your Heavenly Father forgive you your failures* (Matt. 6:14-15, Phillips).

Second Cor. 5:17-21 affirms that God's forgiveness gives freedom to love creatively:

If anyone is in Christ, he is a new creation; the old has gone, the new has come! All this is from God, who reconciled us to himself through Christ and gave us the ministry of reconciliation: that God was reconciling the world to himself in Christ, not counting men's sins against them. And he has committed to us the message of reconciliation. We are therefore Christ's ambassadors, as though God were making his appeal through us. We implore you on Christ's behalf: Be reconciled to God. God made him who had no sin to be sin for us, so that in him we might become the righteousness of God.

Adult children and elderly parents are often unwilling to level dividing walls. Perhaps they do not understand how forgiveness is accomplished.

Survey the Damage

Nehemiah viewed the devastation of Jerusalem before he designed plans to rebuild:

Then I said to them, "You see the trouble we are in: Jerusalem lies in ruins, and its gates have been burned with fire. Come, let us rebuild . . . and we will no longer be in disgrace." I also told them about the gracious hand of my God upon me and what the king had said to me.

They replied, "Let us start rebuilding" (Neh. 2:17-18).

Survey the injury in your life so that needed repairs can occur. Identify what damage has been done. Is there bitterness, depression, difficulty in loving others, exaggerated attempts for acceptance, fear of rejection, feelings of inferiority, hurt feelings, low self-image, pain, perfectionism, inability to trust God, or withdrawal from others?

Who caused the damage in your life? List those with whom you have, or had, conflict. Included may be: mother, father, stepmother, or stepfather.

_____

_____

_____

Acknowledge the Pain from the Damage

Jesus understands the depth of your pain:

He grew up before him like a tender shoot,
and like a root out of dry ground.
He had no beauty or majesty to attract us to him,
nothing in his appearance that we should desire him.
He was despised and rejected by men,
a man of sorrows, and familiar with suffering.
Like one from whom men hide their faces
he was despised, and we esteemed him not.
Surely he took up our infirmities
and carried our sorrows,
yet we considered him stricken by God,
smitten by him, and afflicted.
But he was pierced for our transgressions,
he was crushed for our iniquities;
the punishment that brought us peace was upon him,
and by his wounds we are healed.

(Isa. 53:2-5)

Aching memories cause much suffering in our lives. Feelings are often hidden because of pain. Sincere petitions are prayed: "God, change me," or "Lord, heal the painful memories"—but no healing comes. Repression of feelings hinders healing.

At age 41, Cathie realized she was imprisoned. Circumstances from childhood and teen years had caused incredible pain. She had built her own prison, locked the door, and discounted any means of escape. She was raised in a Christian family, but no one in church knew the terror that filled her home.

When she was three, her Bible-carrying father said, "If you had been born in China, we would have thrown you in the river." She always carried this deep sense of not feeling wanted.

Beatings were common because she did not toe the rigid line. From seventh grade until the end of high school, she was consistently abused sexually by her father. Each time she was told, "I'll beat you to within an inch of your life if you say anything." Cathie knew well what those words meant.

After high school graduation, she met a young man and they married. A family was begun. The abuse ended, but feelings of guilt and shame often surfaced. Cathie had difficulty establishing relationships. She feared letting anyone close enough to discover the family secrets. Through a Christian counselor's guidance, Cathie slowly disclosed the nightmare of her past.

God's Word ministered to her tempest-tossed soul. The words of Psalms 25, 31, and 61 became daily bread. After following through each step to forgiveness, Cathie shared (paraphrasing Charles Wesley), "My chains fell off; my heart is free. / I now go forth to follow Thee." She was now ready for service, including caring for aging parents if God so directed.

Acknowledgment of pain is a difficult step in the forgiveness process. The Holy Spirit brings comfort as painful feelings are courageously expressed.

Some people cannot release their emotions because they find comfort in feeling sorry for themselves. It is easier to have a pity party or blame someone else than to truly acknowledge the pain.

Others casually declare, "Oh, I've forgiven my parents." Instead of working through their unresolved feelings, they accumulate stress-related physical symptoms. Still others truly desire to be free.

Write to Release the Feelings

Remember the upsetting incident, feeling, or conflict. Describe in detail, writing it in letter form. This is NOT given to the offender. It is only a method for deep expression, to help the releasing process.

Example: "Mother, I feel resentment because you never attended any ball games when I was in Little League. You had the time. You just always said, 'I don't like baseball.' It made me feel insignificant and worthless. It was humiliating never having any parental support like the other kids had."

This step's purpose is to recount incidents and experience feelings so that the poison can be released. This is vital in the releasing process of forgiveness.

Burn the letters. Remember, God has promised beauty for ashes (Isa. 61:3).

List Personal Rights That Were Violated

Webster defines a personal right as "something to which one has a just claim." A "right" could be expressed: "I deserve proper nurturing"; "I deserve praise instead of continual criticism"; "I deserve being listened to"; or "I deserve time and attention." List personal rights that were violated:

_____
_____
_____
_____
_____

Yield Those Rights to God

Scripture encourages yielding of rights:

Yield yourselves unto God, as those that are alive from the dead, and your members as instruments of righteousness unto God (Rom. 6:13, KJV).

A decision of the will is involved: "Do I WANT to let go of these feelings?" If so, a prayer can be, "God, I thought this was a basic right I had. I have clutched tightly. I now surrender and release it to You."

List the Wrongs You Have Done to Your Parents

Meditate on these scriptures:

So I strive always to keep my conscience clear before God and man (Acts 24:16).

Our conscience testifies that we have conducted ourselves in the world, and especially in our relations with you, in the holiness and sincerity that are from God. We have done so not according to worldly wisdom but according to God's grace (2 Cor. 1:12).

Keep . . . a clear conscience (1 Pet. 3:16).

Make your list of the wrongs. They might include: impatience, insensitivity, insincerity, intolerance, mistrust, pride, slander, unfairness, unforgiveness, ungratefulness, untruthfulness, or withholding love.

What do you think offended your parents the most? _____

_____

Forgive

And when you stand praying, if you hold anything against anyone, forgive him, so that your Father in heaven may forgive you your sins (Mark 11:25).

Bear with each other and forgive whatever grievances you may have against one another. Forgive as the Lord forgave you (Col. 3:13).

This step seems to be the hardest. When challenged to forgive, responses often are: "I would like to forgive, but . . ."; or "I know I should forgive, but . . ."

Is there anything blocking your ability to love? What is keeping you from forgiving: anger, fear, hurt feelings, insecurity, pride, or stubborn will?

On a sheet of paper write, "My _____ is keeping me from forgiving (name of offender)."

Spend time in prayer with God until you can declare, "I forgive," and there are no "buts" remaining.

Seek Forgiveness

If you are offering your gift at the altar and there remember that your brother has something against you, leave your gift there in front of the altar. First go and be reconciled to your brother; then come and offer your gift (Matt. 5:23-24).

Asking forgiveness clears the conscience. No one can come back and say, "You offended me and never made any effort to make it right."

One approach could be, "I have realized just recently that I was wrong in (list the offense). Will you forgive me?"

Desire Reconciliation

Make every effort to live in peace with all men (Heb. 12:14).

Reconciliation does not mean acceptance of what the violator did. It does not mean what happened has to be denied. Reconciliation means the biblical guideline of seeking peace is being obeyed. It is following the scriptural admonition of rebuilding relationships through unconditional love and acceptance.

Love one another. As I have loved you, so you must love one another. By this all men will know that you are my disciples, if you love one another (John 13:34-35).

Action needs to be taken regardless of feelings. In demonstrating love, tangible expressions should be presented to the violator. These may include prayer, showing appreciation, giving presents, or even long-term care giving.

Now that you have purified yourselves by obeying the truth so that you have sincere love for your brothers, love one another deeply (1 Pet. 1:22).

DISCUSSION QUESTIONS

1. What does Matt. 6:14-15 mean to you?
2. What does reconciliation mean?
3. What is the goal of forgiving?
4. What does Col. 3:12-15 have to say about forgiveness and relationships with your parents?
5. What do the following verses say about real loving? John 13:34-35; 15:9-14; Rom. 13:9; Gal. 5:14; James 2:8; Eph. 5:28-29.

— FOUR —

Dealing with Decisions

*If you want to know what God wants you to do, ask him,
and he will gladly tell you, for he is always ready to give a
bountiful supply of wisdom to all who ask him.*

JAMES 1:5, TLB

"Before Mother's stay in the hospital, she was living on her own and doing fine," a distressed daughter related. "Now her doctor says she will need constant care." Frequently a call for help comes suddenly, often following hospitalization. Decisions must be made within days and sometimes even hours.

When faced with decisions concerning your parents, pray for God's guidance. Second Chronicles, chapter 20, records that a vast army was advancing on Israel. *Alarmed, Jehoshaphat resolved to inquire of the Lord* (v. 3). Jehoshaphat spread the situation out before the Lord (vv. 10-11). He humbled himself before the Lord and said: *We do not know what to do, but our eyes are upon you* (v. 12). God replied: *Do not be afraid; do not be discouraged. . . . [I] will be with you* (v. 17).

As you face the overwhelming decisions, spread them out before God in prayer. Trust the Lord to *guide you in the way of wisdom* (Prov. 4:11).

Find a minister or experienced godly person outside the immediate family to give input. For a reasonable fee, Health Care Concepts at 4006 Arsenal, St. Louis, MO 63116 (314-773-7757) will provide a qualified Christian counselor to help analyze your situation.

Everyone involved in the older adults' living arrangements should participate in the decision-making process. The parents are the ones most affected by the decision. Whenever possible, they should have the final say. Adult children, grandchildren, and perhaps brothers and sisters should have an opportunity to voice opinions about the arrangements, especially if their lives will be affected. The following steps will help guide your family through the process of finding the best possible care.

Steps

Define the Situation

Assess what is happening now. Try to determine what the situation will be in one year and then within three years.

- What is the dependency stage of the aging parent?
  Minimal. Physical strength beginning to wane.
  Partially dependent. Others must help.
  Total dependency. Cannot function unaided.

- What is the mental condition?
    Normal forgetfulness
    Impairment of mental abilities
    Unaware of self and others
- What is their physical health status?
    Ambulatory
    Wheelchair
    Bed bound
- Is help needed with activities of daily living?
    Eating
    Dressing and undressing
    Personal hygiene
    Light housekeeping
    Getting in and out of bed
    Walking
    Performing medical self-care tasks
    Writing
    Preparing meals
    Transportation
- Rehabilitation services needed?
    Speech
    Physical therapy
- What financial resources are available?
    Automobile
    Bank account
    Pension benefits
    Royalty contracts
    Real estate
    Stocks and bonds
    Trust deeds
- What insurance coverage is available?
    Life
    Health
- What are the financial liabilities?
    Debts
    Mortgages
    Property taxes
- What is the primary caregiver's health?
    Poor
    Good
    Excellent
- Support from other family members?
    Partial
    Wholehearted
    Local or distant
- Are parents willing to change present life-style?
- What is the adult child's disposition toward a different life-style?
    Negative

Hesitant
Positive
- What is the duration of the commitment?
Months
Years
Unknown

Prioritize Needs

Consider the problem. Make a list of needs—health care, daily living activities, and financial.

List Creative Alternatives

Read chapter 5, "Overview of Options." List all creative housing alternatives suitable for the aging parents. Eliminate solutions that won't work. Sort through remaining possibilities with your family members, and remember their individual needs.

Take Action

Only God knows the unknown future. Continue to seek His will until you have inner conviction and peace, then take action.

Guidelines

- People do not age identically. Each situation should be assessed independently. Look at your loved one as an individual, not an older adult stereotype.
- When deterioration symptoms are recognized and a more structured environment is needed, assist aging parents with making a decision while they still are competent. The adult child may need to clarify issues and give advice. But the privilege of deciding for oneself is important. They should have the right to be consulted about their future.
- Take time to listen to aging parents. Observe the entire situation. Listen and learn about their hopes, fears, anxieties, and plans for the future.
- The ultimate goal is to help parents remain in their own home and stay as independent as possible.
- What is right for one family may not be possible for another. Don't base decisions on someone else's circumstances.
- Anyone considering becoming a caregiver must be healthy. Consider the present work load. Estimate the likelihood of increasing dependency and what this will mean. The caregiver must be able to physically, mentally, and spiritually deal with the changes.
- If time is needed to make a decision and adequately prepare, arrange temporary admission to a convalescent or nursing home.
- Have a backup plan ready. Circumstances change, and care giving may not be possible indefinitely. A backup plan also should include respite care for extended weekends or evenings out.
- Bonnie Jamison's book, *Take Me Home*, offers insight into the difficult decision-making process. Write the author for an autographed copy: 3 Great Bridge Ct., Medford, NJ 08055.

DISCUSSION QUESTIONS

1. Why are hospitalizations often traumatic for older adults?

2. How does prayer help when dealing with decisions?

3. Why is it important to seek counsel from a godly person when faced with decisions?

4. Why is it important to involve the entire family in the decision-making process?

5. How are older adults stereotyped?

Full Circle
by Marilyn Hamilton

It seems the roles of parent and child
   Are reversed during the later years.
Now it's me giving comfort and care
   To the one who used to dry my tears.

The hands that helped me take my first steps,
   Now hold firmly to me as we walk.
The voice that patiently taught me speech,
   Now trembles in an effort to talk.

The one whose memory used to challenge mine
   To learn and remember each detail;
Now struggles to recall my birthdate
   And my children's names, to no avail.

I've heard people claim it's not their job
   To care for their parents who are old.
They pay someone else to do that task
   And keep from putting their life on hold.

I contend it's not a sacrifice,
   But a privilege to be giving;
To parents who not only gave life,
   But made it a life well worth living.

─── FIVE ───

Overview of Options

Give careful thought to housing choices before an emergency forces this decision. Options are scanned in this chapter.

Independent Living

Consumer Housing Information Service for Seniors (CHISS) volunteers are available for home visits with older persons. They assist with specific problems and provide detailed community housing-option information.

The volunteers are trained to tackle housing issues. These can range from searching for a continuing-care home that will take a healthy husband and his frail wife to finding a program that will repair rotting back-porch steps.

For information write: CHISS, AARP Program Dept., 1909 K St. N.W., Washington, DC 20049.

The American Association of Homes for the Aging (AAHA) also answers questions concerning senior housing. Check your phone book for an AAHA branch in your area, or write for free brochures to: AAHA, 1129 20th St. N.W., Suite 400, Washington, DC 20036. Include a self-addressed, stamped, business-sized envelope.

Staying in Own Home

Being able to stay in their own dwelling is the first choice for most older adults. This option works if the individual can perform daily tasks. Privacy, independence, and personal satisfaction contribute to a high quality of life.

Your parents may be able to remain in their own home with assistance. Many services are available for those living independently:

Adopt a Grandkid—Check with your parents' church for a teenager or adult to do chores such as running errands or light housekeeping. The local Boy/Girl Scouts often assist the older adults in the neighborhood.

"Aging Network Services" (ANS)—ANS provides a private service specifically designed to address problems confronting adult children with aging parents living in other areas. A plan is designed to maintain independence to the greatest extent for aging loved ones. The staff works with a nationwide network of qualified clinical social workers who assess the parents' condition and arrange for necessary services. For an introduction to this service write: ANS, 4400 East-West Hwy., Suite 907, Bethesda, MD 20814; or call 301-657-4329.

"American Association of Retired Persons" (AARP)—For individuals over 50, AARP provides information on services and money savers. It also publishes *Modern Maturity* magazine and the AARP *Bulletin*. For information on the reasonable membership requirements, write: AARP, P.O. Box 199, Long Beach, CA 90801-9989.

Assistive Telephone Devices—Special telephone equipment is available for individuals with hearing, motion, speech, or vision impairments. For information contact the National Special Needs Center: toll-free, 800-233-1222.

Before-You-Leave Chart—Post a chart by your parents' door. This is a list of things that should be done before leaving home, such as: Are lights off? Is stove off? Is iron unplugged? Are windows closed? Are keys in hand?

"CARE-Line"—If your parent is far away and needs the loving support of the Body of Christ, call CARE-Line, toll-free, 800-821-2154 (in Missouri, 816-333-7000, ext. 2440).

Emergency Medical Information—If your parent has a specific medical problem, it might be wise to secure an emergency medical metal tag. For a free brochure, contact: Medic Alert Foundation International, Turlock, CA 95381-1009.

A wallet-size health information card also is available. Send a stamped, self-addressed business envelope to: Health and Safety Education Division, Metropolitan Life Insurance Company, One Madison Ave., New York, NY 10010.

Home Environment Adaptations—Many older persons can maintain independence in their own homes with environment adaptations. For a free informational booklet on making your parents' home fit their needs, write: AARP, Consumer Affairs, 1909 K St. N.W., Washington, DC 20049. Ask for *The Do*Able Renewable Home*.

Home Healthcare—Home healthcare generally involves regular home visits by a registered nurse, a licensed practical nurse, a home health aide, or a nutritionist. This type of care is usually provided only with a doctor's recommendation.

According to the Bureau of Consumer Protection, an estimated 8,000 agencies provide some form of home care. Be sure the agency under consideration is in compliance with state requirements for certification and is accredited.

Home Safety—Are your parents' surroundings safe? Examine their home using the "Home Safety Checklist" (Appendix, p. 89).

Homemaking Services—Homemaking services are designed to help elderly parents with light housekeeping, laundry, food shopping, personal care, and meal preparation. The extent of services provided depends on the needs. Fees vary accordingly.

Services can be arranged through an agency or on an individual basis through newspaper advertising or word of mouth. Always check references before you hire anyone to work in your parents' home.

"Lifeline System"—If a parent might be unable to call for needed help, consider the Lifeline System. A button, worn around the neck, can be pressed to sound an alarm at a nearby agency, often a hospital. When the

alarm is sounded, the agency dials the wearer's home. If there is no response, the representative phones the family member or neighbor pre-arranged to check. Call toll-free 800-331-7972 for the nearest Lifeline System office.

Weigh the benefits of renting a system versus buying. Make sure the monitoring-station staff is adequate, is supervised, keeps up-to-date records, and is available around the clock. Test the device in the home before buying.

Maintenance and Repair—Many communities provide a home maintenance and repair service for the elderly. These programs are often administered by local neighborhood improvement or social service agencies. For a nominal annual fee, someone will go to the home once a year. This person will do repair work and be available to assist whenever there is an emergency, such as a frozen pipe or a broken window. Some provide free labor for repairs, but the homeowner may be asked to furnish the necessary materials.

"Meals on Wheels"—Meals on Wheels is a program available for seniors who have difficulty preparing their own meals or do not have transportation to a grocery store. Once a day, volunteers deliver nutritious hot lunches and cold food for the evening meal to the home.

Pen Pals—International Pen Friends have members in 153 countries. When suggesting a pen pal, this organization pays close attention to hobbies, special interests, and age-groups. Admission fee is low. For information write: International Pen Friends, P.O. Box 190065, Homecrest Station, Brooklyn, NY 11229-0001.

Pet Companions—Pets are beneficial for the older adult. Emotionally an animal provides companionship and a sense of being needed. People talk to animals. This practice invigorates mental abilities. Providing pet care demonstrates the owner is needed and provides meaning for life. Preparing the pet's meal, getting it outside, going for a walk, and petting all provide exercise. Several medical studies have actually proven that pets can improve the mental and physical well-being of the elderly, even to the extent of helping to lower high blood pressure and speeding recovery from illness.

Pets for the Elderly Program works in cooperation with animal shelters in a select number of cities across the country. Their goal is to bring senior citizens and homeless pets together in mutually beneficial relationships. Through funding from Pets for People, local humane organizations can provide pets for the elderly at no initial cost. The program covers the cost of adoption fees, initial veterinary visits, spaying or neutering, pet supplies, and a supply of pet foods. For information write: Purina Pets for People Program, Checkerboard Square 6T, St. Louis, MO 63164.

Dogs are also trained to help people with hearing problems—to alert them to the ringing of the phone or doorbell. If a parent is living alone, could benefit from this service, and would enjoy the companionship of an animal, further information is available from: Canine Companions for Independence, P.O. Box 446, Santa Rosa, CA 95402-0446.

"Pets in Families with Older Parents" (chap. 13 in *Help! I'm Parenting My Parents*, ed. Jamia Jacobsen [Indianapolis: Benchmark Press, 1988]) should be read before securing a pet.

Postal Alert—The postal service provides a program called Postal Alert for the older adult who lives alone. A sign on the mailbox says, "If my mail is stacking up, please call the police department so that they can check on my welfare." A free brochure is available from the post office.

Senior Citizen Centers—Social and recreational opportunities are provided in senior citizen centers. They can be a fulfilling outlet for older adults who have the energy and abilities to participate.

Stamps by Mail—The United States Postal Service now sells stamps by phone. Call toll-free 800-782-6724. The order will be delivered in three to five business days. Stamps must be charged, and there's a $3.00 service fee.

Telephone Reassurance—Under Telephone Reassurance, a volunteer calls each day of the week at a prearranged time. Check different headings in the telephone directory, such as Telecare, Care Ring, Ring-a-Day, Good Neighbor, or Phone Alert League (PAL).

Ask the pastor of your parents' church if they provide daily contact for their homebound members. Often senior adult groups are organized with phone checkup systems.

Transportation Program—Most communities offer an older adult transportation system for errands and appointments. Check the heading Senior Citizen Service Organizations in the yellow pages.

Visually Impaired Aids—VisAids Inc. (102-09 Jamaica Ave., P.O. Box 26, Richmond Hill, NY 11418) offers aids and appliances for the visually impaired and physically challenged. Call toll-free 800-346-9579 for a free catalog.

Moving to a Smaller Place

Aging parents may need to consider a place less demanding for maintenance or more accessible to transportation. Possibilities are a mobile home, apartment, or condominium. Senior citizen complexes are usually located near shopping centers, transportation lines, and other community services.

A Guide to Renting an Apartment is a free booklet available from State Farm Insurance Companies, Public Relations Department, One State Farm Plaza, Bloomington, IL 61710-0001.

If thinking about purchasing a mobile home, write: Consumer Information Center-V, P.O. Box 100, Pueblo, CO 81002. Ask for *How to Buy a Manufactured (Mobile) Home* booklet, No. 429V. Send 50 cents.

Moving to a Retirement Community

Retirement community houses are usually small and built on one floor. This arrangement provides integration of housing and services in a noninstitutional environment.

Shared Housing May Be a Possibility

Shared housing is an arrangement in which two or more unrelated people combine their belongings, resources, and finances to share a dwelling. Each person has a bedroom but shares the living room, dining room, and kitchen.

Shared housing can produce rental income or simply mean an exchange of services. Possibilities for shared-housing partners are a younger couple, a college student, or several elderly people.

Compatibility is a primary concern if considering this option. Contact local churches for Christian individuals who might be interested in shared housing.

Questions for consideration:

- Will neighborhood zoning laws permit two or more unrelated people to share a home?
- Will income received have any effect on Supplementary Security Income?

For information on shared housing programs in your region, contact: Shared Housing Resource Center, 6344 Greene St., Philadelphia, PA 19144 (212-848-1220).

Share-a-Home interviewing forms are available for $2.50 to cover postage and handling. Write: Project HOPE Director, P.O. Box 3130, Memphis, TN 38173-0130.

Semi-independent Living

Semi-independent living is housing with services for the older adult needing help with routine activities. If services such as shopping, meal preparation, household tasks, and personal care cannot be brought into the home, a setting must be located to provide them.

Board and Care Home (Residential Care Home)

Some people are interested enough in older adults to receive them in their homes. Often it is a situation where the individual in charge has an elderly person living with them already.

This concept may be called adult foster care in some areas. The home must be licensed to operate. Someone lives in the home 24 hours a day and provides services.

Quality of services provided in board and care homes varies. If your parents are accustomed to certain cleanliness standards or have other requirements, select a home that satisfies their needs. Before entering into a contract, make an assessment of services offered so that expectations will be met.

Congregate Housing

Congregate housing can be a high-rise building or a clustered-housing approach. Each has a self-contained living unit, with kitchenette, bathroom, and living room-bedroom combination.

Professional staff are on the premises. Supportive services are offered such as housekeeping, transportation, social activities, and meal packages.

Congregate homes are not nursing homes. Skilled nursing or medical care is not offered.

Usually residents pay monthly lease fees. Other services are offered on an optional or pay-as-you-go basis.

Without requiring your parents to give up their privacy and independence, congregate housing provides a source of companionship and group involvement. A sense of security is built in, knowing assistance is available when needed.

Congregate facilities are listed in the yellow pages under Senior Citizens' Service Organizations or Retirement and Lifecare Communities and Homes. For further information contact a local office on aging.

Continuing Care Retirement Community (CCRC)

In a continuing care retirement community, residents contract for services relating to their living arrangement. This can range from independent maintenance to long-term nursing care.

Initially, the older adult may live in a private unit. Meals may be shared in a central dining area. If health deteriorates, the resident may move to an area within the community that provides assisted living and nursing care.

Continuing care communities are usually more expensive than board and care homes and congregate housing. They generally require a substantial entrance fee, as well as monthly charges. Continuing care communities represent a lifetime commitment.

Carefully screen the program and reputation for quality of care. Obtain a copy of the contract. Understand what services are being engaged. It would be wise to seek professional legal advice before accepting this arrangement.

Plan ahead. The better communities have long waiting lists.

For a list of CCRCs in your area, check the *National Continuing Care Directory* (Ann Trueblood Raper, editor) from the library. This reference book has comprehensive information on retirement facilities offering prepaid contracts for long-term care.

Living with Family

It may be your parents have been living independently. Your lives are separate but meshed through occasional visits, letters, and phone calls. Then, at some point, circumstances change, infirmities develop, or new fears are expressed. The parents are no longer able to care for themselves or afford one of the previous alternatives. For many adult children, having a parent live with family is the more viable option.

Creative Alternatives

Several possibilities exist for living with family:
- Adult children and grandchildren move into the older adult's home.
- Older adult relocates in the child's home with living quarters separate, yet a part of the home.
- An accessory apartment is created from space already available within the house, providing a complete living unit, including separate kitchen. Check the local zoning commission for community regulations.
- ECHO (Elder Cottage Housing Opportunity) unit stands separate from the main house or is attached by a breezeway or porch. Place-

ment depends upon zoning restrictions and special-use permits. Such units are practical because when no longer needed, they can be sold and moved from the property. This idea has greater acceptance in rural or semi-rural communities.

Observations

Three-generational living works best when the elderly parents' living quarters are separate, yet a part of the home. Grandparents can rest, read, or retire as desired. They can listen to their choice of radio or TV programs, at their selected volume. They also can join the family for fellowship or lend a hand with chores.

When strong ties of affection exist between adult children and their parents, the experience of living together can be enriching, though toilsome, for both generations. Lives will be altered, whether the parent moves into the adult child's home or into one that is nearby. In any situation, the two generations basically become one family unit.

Prepare carefully. Become familiar with services and supplies available; learn needed nursing skills; start the organizational process; begin studying about specific illnesses your parents have; and make necessary practical changes around the house.

Bringing parents into the adult child's home may mean setting aside personal dreams and developing a servant's heart. Prepare to give love and care that only an adult child can offer the needy parent. Assist as long as possible. Understand that eventually, under certain circumstances, the next option for consideration may be a nursing home.

Nursing Home

Considerations

Deciding if and when to place a parent in a nursing home is a wrenching dilemma. The bottom line is doing what is best for the parent.

A physician may recommend sending the aging parent to a nursing home. Do not take such a suggestion as an order. Consider these questions:

- Is this individual a geriatric specialist?
- Is the doctor acquainted with your parent as a total person?
- Is the advice based on the best interests for the entire family?
- Is the recommendation being made simply because the physician has no other alternatives to suggest?

Options

The two basic types of nursing facilities are Intermediate Care Facility (ICF) and Skilled Nursing Facility (SNF). Both are certified to meet federal standards. However, only SNF is state licensed and federally certified as a provider of Medicare and Medicaid programs. The SNF is similar to a hospital and has 24-hour skilled nursing care provided. The ICF is for people who cannot live alone but do not need round-the-clock care. They need personal care services, which are provided in the ICF.

The SNF is often appropriate for short-term rehabilitation following surgery or serious illness.

Choosing a Home

Intense research is necessary to choose the right home. Question everything, such as quality of care, certification of staff, food service, and available activities for residents. As with CCRCs, the top-notch facilities have long waiting lists. Planning ahead will avoid major problems that can result from trying to place a parent in a hurry.

Finding the right place often is difficult. Names of desirable homes may be obtained from other families in the community, a doctor, or a minister. Your area agency on aging is a good source of assistance. Other sources of referral include the local hospital's social services department and the local or state health department. A "Nursing Home Checklist" is available in this book (Appendix, p. 97).

If a nursing home is certified to receive Medicare and Medicaid reimbursement, it will have passed a rigorous inspection by the state licensing agency to see that it complies with federal and state regulations. Check thoroughly that the home under consideration is properly licensed and accredited.

All nursing homes are expensive; Medicare or Medicaid will not pay for all expenses. Know your state's rules, regulations, and reimbursement schedules. Usually, long-term care insurance defrays only a portion of the cost. Most residents pay their own way until assets run out and Medicaid coverage takes over.

Understand the financial arrangements:

- What does the government (Medicare or Medicaid) pay?
- What is covered by supplemental insurance?
- What do you pay out of pocket?

Obtain the daily rate figures. Know specifically what this does, and does not, include. List all extra charges. A lawyer should review the agreement before signing.

Solving Problems

The best way for families to assure quality care for an elderly relative in a nursing home is for family members and friends to continue to be involved with the older person through frequent visiting and good communication with the nursing home staff. If a question or problem arises regarding care of your parent, the first step in resolving the issue is to talk to the nursing staff or the social worker. If the issue continues to be of concern, then talk to the nursing home administrator.

If these steps do not resolve the issue, contact the nursing home ombudsman who serves the community. The ombudsman office works with nursing home residents and families to negotiate a satisfactory resolution to questions or problems that have surfaced. There is no charge for their services. For the ombudsman's address, contact your state agency on aging.

Making a Smooth Transition

Admitting a loved one into a nursing home is stressful for everyone involved. Some homes have a social worker or nurse specialist who conducts preadmission group sessions for family members.

Ease the transition by accompanying your parent on moving day. Make the room personal with family photos, plants, favorite mementos, and decorative items.

Patricia Rushford reminds adult children that "it is not a 'sin' to place your elderly parent in a nursing home. The sin begins when an elderly parent is 'dumped' into an institution and forgotten" (*The Help, Hope, and Cope Book for People with Aging Parents* [Old Tappan, N.J.: Fleming H. Revell Co., 1985]).

Visit regularly. The presence of family members creates a more personal atmosphere and offers reassurance that someone still cares. It also sends a message to the nursing home staff that they must regularly account for quality of care provided.

❖ ❖ ❖

DISCUSSION QUESTIONS

1. Where are your parents now living?

2. How does geography affect relationships with our parents?

3. How would you feel about having to place a parent in a nursing home?

4. If an unexpected crisis occurred with a parent, what other options besides a nursing home would your family have?

—————— SIX ——————

Answers to Anxieties

*God is . . . an ever-present help in trouble. Therefore we
will not fear.* PS. 46:1-2

Deciphering laws and understanding financial matters pertaining to older
adults can make you feel as agitated as a drop of water on a hot griddle.
The background information in this chapter can help you untangle knotty
legal and money matters.

Legal Issues

Will

A will is a legal document stating how to dispose of property after
death. It determines how the estate will be distributed, who the personal
representative will be, and when the distribution will take place.

An estimated two out of three people die without leaving a will. This
means state laws direct how assets are distributed to beneficiaries. Help
parents understand it is worth the time and expense to draw up a will. In
this way, their money and belongings can be distributed as they desire. Be
sure parents draw up their wills while they are still competent.

In preparation for drawing up a will, parents should inventory their
assets, including personal property, real estate, and business investments.
Subtract liabilities. An indication of desired distribution should also be
made.

A will should be stored in a safe place, with copies in a separate location. It should be reviewed and updated every few years. If there is a
move to another state, the will must be reviewed because states differ in
their laws regarding wills.

Contact the Planned Giving Department of your general church organization for forms, brochures, and guidance concerning drawing up a
will.

Consult a trusted licensed attorney. A lawyer's guidance in drawing
up a will is invaluable. Laws vary from state to state and change over
time. Failure to follow all rules and regulations may make a will invalid.

Legal Counsel for the Elderly (LCE) offers a free legal hotline service
for older Americans. Check your phone directory for a local number or
write: LCE, 1909 K St. N.W., Washington, DC 20049.

The Simple Will Book, written in 1986 by Denis Clifford (Nolo Press,
950 Parker St., Berkeley, CA 94701), is a valuable resource containing tear-

out forms. It is available from Nolo Press by calling toll-free 800-922-NO-LO.

Living Will

A living will should be seriously considered. This is a precise directive to physicians regarding medical decisions parents have made for when they become unable to make their wishes known. It states which treatments are desired and whether pain medication is to be administered once treatment is withdrawn.

A living will is not to be confused with a will, which is a legal declaration of a person's wishes as to the disposition of property after death occurs. A living will specifies desires regarding the use of life-sustaining treatment in the event of a terminal illness.

A proxy and alternate should be chosen who will abide by the wishes of the living will. This representation may be needed in a hospital or court.

A living will is legal only as advice in many states. Check with your parents' lawyer, state health department, or state department on aging for detailed and current information. Some states also require a durable power of attorney for healthcare.

Before parents write a living will, they should spend time in prayer and seek godly counsel from their pastor. Life-support measures should be discussed with their family doctor to make sure the document will be respected.

The living will should be signed before two witnesses who are neither relatives nor proxies. Keep the original in your parents' "Important Papers" file. Give copies to the physician and lawyer or estate executor.

Pulitzer prize-winning reporter B. D. Colen details exactly how to write and videotape a legally sanctioned document in his book, *The Essential Guide to a Living Will* (New York: Prentice Hall, 1991). Included in his book are copies of the living wills for each of the 41 states, plus the District of Columbia, that had a living will as of October 1990.

Living Trust

A living trust is a popular concept. People are able to transfer their assets into a trust while they are alive. This enables their assets to be bequeathed to family members and others without probate expenses. It can also result in substantial savings in inheritance taxes at the time of death. A revocable living trust is an estate-planning tool that may accomplish what a will won't.

Trust

A trust is a legal agreement whereby title to assets (e.g., cash, stocks, bonds, real estate, etc.) is transferred to a trustee. The trustee's responsibilities are outlined in the trust document and normally include: asset investment, distribution of trust income during the person's lifetime, and distribution of the assets at the person's death. A trust is a supplement to, not a replacement of, a will.

Power of Attorney

The time may come when a parent is unable to handle affairs. A parent may only be incapacitated in regard to handling financial affairs but still able to make healthcare decisions. Maybe parents can handle their own daily finances but need assistance with investments. Advance planning will eliminate court proceedings.

Power of attorney documents are inexpensive and easy to execute. A conventional form may be purchased from an office supply store. Sample documents are included in *The Power of Attorney Book,* by Denis Clifford (Nolo Press; see earlier this chapter).

Have the document notarized. Planning ahead eliminates the possibility of a parent being sick or unable to sign. Should this occur, call a bank, real estate office, or lawyer for the name of a notary who can go to the parent.

The forms should be witnessed by at least two people, even if not required by law. Witnessing in this way promotes acceptability. It is preferable to use individuals who are not relatives or anyone who might benefit from the parent's death.

Financial Matters

Insurance

Parents should have two types of insurance: life insurance (the policy should cover funeral and other financial needs of remaining spouse) and private health insurance (Medicare and Medicaid does not cover all costs). If you are handling a parent's financial affairs, contact their insurance agent. Make sure all policies are paid and in force.

Medicare is a limited federal convalescent health insurance program for individuals over the age of 65. Medicare information is available through a local Social Security office.

Medicaid is a cooperative federal-state insurance program providing services for low-income people. Guidelines vary by state.

If a parent has an insurance policy that can't be located, the **American Council of Life Insurance** (ACLI) will try to determine the issuing company and trace the policy for you. Send a stamped, self-addressed, legal-size envelope to: Contact Policy Search, ACLI, 1001 Pennsylvania Ave. N.W., Washington, DC 20004.

Because of nursing home costs, families should obtain information on **long-term care insurance.** Shop around and compare the prices and terms of various policies. *The Consumer's Guide to Long-Term Care Insurance* is a free guide that helps in comparing policies, benefits, and costs. Write: Company Services, Health Insurance Association of America, 1001 Pennsylvania Ave. N.W., Washington, DC 20004-2599. Include a self-addressed label and specify publication No. 1262.

The booklet *Your Medicare Handbook* may be obtained from the nearest Social Security Administration office.

Check the library for a current copy of *The Complete and Easy Guide to Social Security and Medicare,* by Faustine F. Jehle.

The Department of Health and Human Services Inspector General's Hotline assists people who have been overbilled or billed for services not rendered through Medicare or Medicaid. Call toll-free 800-368-5779 (in Maryland, 301-579-0724).

A workable system will be needed for keeping track of the complicated health insurance business. Months can pass between the time service is rendered and payment received. Accurate records must be kept so that you are not lost in the maze of figures. The amount of unreimbursed medical expenses is needed for tax purposes. Perhaps you would like to use the "Health Insurance Record" (Appendix, p. 87).

Social Security

Social Security checks are not automatically sent. Application must be made for benefits.

A representative payee is someone who serves as an agent in receiving and depositing Social Security checks. An adult child can apply for representative's payee status at a local Social Security office.

Social Security pays a death benefit to the surviving spouse. The nearest office should be notified and a request made for an application for death benefits.

Contact the local Social Security office for updated information on procedures; write the Social Security Administration, Public Information, Security Blvd., Baltimore, MD 21235; or call the administration's toll-free telephone service: 800-234-5772.

Supplemental Social Security

Supplemental Security Income (SSI) is a federally funded program that pays a monthly allowance to financially needy individuals age 65 and over, or those who are blind or disabled. Eligibility for SSI is determined by the total value of an applicant's assets and income.

For more information, contact the local Social Security office or write: Social Security Administration, Public Information, Security Blvd., Baltimore, MD 21235. Ask for free SSI brochures.

If an eligible person moves to another person's household, his basic Supplemental Security Income is cut by one-third, regardless of the actual value of the support and maintenance. Any change in the circumstances of an SSI beneficiary should be reported immediately to the Social Security office.

Taxes

Write Internal Revenue Service, CADC, P.O. Box 9903, Bloomington, IL 61799, for a free copy of the publication *Tax Information for Older Americans* (Publication No. 554). This includes blank tax forms in larger print and general tax requirements.

Protecting Older Americans Against Overpayment of Taxes is a free brochure available from Documents, Senate Special Committee on Aging, SH-628, U.S. Senate, Washington, DC 20510-6400. This provides checklists to follow for making itemized deductions to ensure there is no overpayment on federal income tax.

J. R. Lasser's *Your Income Tax* (Prentice Hall Press) is a perennial best-seller. This is a comprehensive, accurate handbook on tax advice and year-round financial planning. The local library normally will have copies of this by November.

Find out if a parent qualifies for earned income tax credit (EITC) or senior tax credit.

February 1 through April 15, volunteers from AARP's Tax-Aide Program are available at locations around the country to help low- and moderate-income older taxpayers file federal, state, and local tax returns. Call the toll-free IRS number listed previously, and ask for the location of the nearest AARP Tax Counseling for the Elderly Program.

The Problem Resolution Office (PRO) ensures taxpayers they have somewhere to turn when normal IRS procedures fail. Consider PRO if a parent has problems with missing refund checks, an amended tax return is filed but never acknowledged, or continued billings are made after a tax has been paid. Under this program, a specific IRS employee monitors a taxpayer's complaints or questions until they are resolved. If needed, call the local IRS office and ask for the Problem Resolution Office.

It may be necessary to file a final return when a parent dies. Ask the IRS to help with this if needed.

Check with a local IRS office to see if any tax credits are available for a working adult who helps pay for the care of a dependent parent incapable of self-care. Detailed information on dependent care tax credit can be obtained by calling the national IRS toll-free number: 800-829-3676. (Service hours: Monday-Friday, 8 A.M. to 4:30 P.M., Eastern time.) Ask for Publication No. 907, *Tax Information for Persons with Handicaps or Disabilities.*

Checking and Saving Accounts

At least one adult child's name should be on all checking and savings accounts. If a parent becomes incapacitated, the family needs access to these funds.

Funeral Prefinance

Proceed with care in arranging for prepayment funeral plans. Not all are desirable:

• The actual total price of the funeral is rarely guaranteed.

• You may needlessly tie up your money with no interest for many years.

• The contract may be irrevocable, with no interest earned on payments.

• A funeral director may suggest regular time payments. This is risky and illegal in many states if the money is not placed in a state-supervised trust fund. If you die before the entire amount is paid off, the mortuary may not honor the contract. You may not be able to redeem your money if you want to cancel.

• The funeral home may be sold, closed, or go bankrupt.

Information about prepaid funeral plans can be obtained by writing: Continental Association of Funeral and Memorial Societies, 2001 South St. N.W., Suite 530, Washington, DC 20009.

For information on state laws affecting the purchase of prepaid funerals, check with your state funeral board, insurance commissioner, or attorney general.

Alternative Funeral Prefinance Programs

● Special savings account to cover funeral cost. Talk with a cooperative funeral director for an estimate of funeral expenses. Open an account designated specifically for this purpose. The account needs to be set up so that a parent has full control while alive. Then the adult child or a designated party can draw out the money upon the parent's death.

● Life insurance policy that covers anticipated funeral expenses. Upon death, the policy provides the needed funds.

DISCUSSION QUESTIONS

1. What is a will?

2. Why is a will so important?

3. Why is a lawyer's guidance invaluable when drawing up a will?

4. What is the difference between a will and a living will?

5. Cite examples when a power of attorney might be necessary.

6. State reasons why prepaid funeral plans may not be the best option.

7. Why is it important to talk with your parents bfore a crisis occurs to learn their wishes in the event of mental or physical incapacity?

8. Why is it important to know the location of your parents' important documents?

—————SEVEN—————

Observant to Organization

Live life, then, with a due sense of responsibility, not as men who do not know the meaning of life but as <u>those who</u> <u>do.</u> Make the best use of your time, despite all the evils of these days. EPH. 5:15-16, PHILLIPS, underlines in text

Making Life Easier

Have you heard the phrase "Running around like a chicken with its head cut off"? I never understood this until visiting relatives. Forever implanted in my memory is watching my uncle chop off a chicken's head, toss the body on the ground, and seeing that headless body run around!

The caregiver's life must be systematized to survive. Otherwise, running from one responsibility to another will resemble the activity of the headless chicken.

Everyone has the same 24 hours to use. The number of hours does not determine what you accomplish. It is how you use those hours. "Some people count time; others make time count," an old adage says. The Psalmist prayed, "Teach us to number our days and recognize how few they are; help us to spend them as we should" (90:12, TLB).

Do you ever feel pressured by time? Perhaps you are either doing the wrong thing or doing the right thing in the wrong way. Organizing is arranging life in an orderly way. Such efforts result in additional time. The following are ideas to help save time, organize for efficiency, and make life easier.

Daily Care Plan

Complete the "Daily Care Plan" (Appendix, p. 81) for your parent. This will:
- Help set priorities for efficient care giving
- Give a complete picture of the necessary routine
- Lessen explanations when someone else is in charge

Menu Planning

Talk with all family members about their favorite food dishes. Set up a "Monthly Meal Planner" for lunch and dinner. Breakfast is easier and does not need to be included in this plan. Use this outline each month to save time in meal planning (Appendix, p. 95).

Keep alert for easy-to-make recipes. File them and occasionally add to the "Monthly Meal Planner." For a booklet of *Quick and Easy Recipes* write to Parent Care Publications, P.O. Box 216, Bethany, OK 73008.

Important Papers on File

Have a file on parents that includes: automobile registration, bank books, birth certificates, "Funeral Planning Form" (Appendix, p. 83), insurance policies, living will, marriage certificate, "Medical History Chart" (Appendix, p. 91), "Medicine Chart" (Appendix, p. 93), photocopy of will and notation of location of original, power of attorney, recent IRS records, and securities such as stocks and bonds.

Medical History Chart and Medicine Chart

Complete a "Medical History Chart" and "Medicine Chart" for your parents (see above). This will save valuable time at the doctor's office, hospital, emergency room, or home health service.

Funeral Planning Forms

Fill out a "Funeral Planning Form" for both parents (see above). Xerox copies and place in their "Important Papers" file.

Prescription Renewals

When filling or refilling a prescription, mark a calendar several days before it needs to be renewed. This eliminates last-minute trips to the pharmacy when the medicine runs out.

Birthdays

Precious time is often spent deciding what birthday present to buy a parent. It is often difficult to buy for the older adult. Gift ideas include:

- Airline ticket
- Bible on cassette
- Change kitty for those who purchase a daily newspaper, use a bus, or pay for doing laundry
- Drink items such as instant coffee, tea bags, instant hot chocolate, instant spiced cider, or small juices
- Favorite food items
- Fresh flowers
- Fruit arranged in a small basket
- Gift certificates—beauty shop, restaurant, store
- Labor coupon for someone else to wash windows or fix broken items
- Large-print books
- Magazine subscription to fit recipient's interest
- Original artwork by children or grandchildren
- Photo albums or collage frames
- Stamped envelopes with return address printed or typed on
- Stationery (lined) or postcards
- Telephone certificates
- Telephone kitty—an envelope or jar with money designated for telephone calls to family
- Tickets—musical or sporting event

● Updated pictures of family

The White House sends birthday greetings to anyone 80 years or older. Send the parent's name and address at least 30 days before a birthday to: Greetings Office, The White House, 1600 Pennsylvania Ave., Washington, DC 20500.

Before a new year begins, list individuals to whom you will be sending birthday cards. Take the list to the store and purchase all cards. Address the envelopes. With pencil, in the upper right corner, write the date the card should be mailed. When the day approaches, write a note, sign the card, and attach a stamp.

Correspondence

Use prestamped postcards for answering mail. These are available from the post office in any quantity for the price of the stamp. Prestamp the return address on all cards at once. Then only a few moments are required to write a message and address. This is an efficient method for maintaining correspondence and attending to the multivarious care-giving responsibilities.

Direct Deposit

If elderly parents are not using direct deposit for their pension checks, consider setting it up. Financial institutions have applications for electronic funds transfer (EFT). Required information includes: claim number shown on each check; suffix under the claim number; type of payment; name of beneficiaries (payees on checks); and checking or savings account number. Check the monthly bank statement to be sure the transfer appears.

Easy Access of Supplies

For parents who are immobile or can't get around easily, have needed items within reach. These include eyeglasses, books, water, and toilet articles. Keep medical, personal, and cleaning supplies in the room where they are used. Make a list of items that need to be replaced soon. Purchase them on your next shopping trip.

Portable Phone

What a time-saver this is! While talking on the phone, you can cook, iron, or give care.

The Tele-Consumer Hotline (toll-free, 800-332-1124) will send a free fact sheet on how to choose a phone and what to do when the phone does not work.

Automatic Dial Telephone

Even the least expensive models of automatic dial telephones have enough channels to preset important phone numbers. The caregiver or parents need only push a button for fire, police, doctor, etc. Most units have redial. If the line is busy and the call does not go through, one button will redial the number automatically.

Record Telephone Numbers

Write down a telephone number after looking it up. Put the name and number in an address book, Rolodex, or appropriate file. The moments it takes to record it will be made up by the time saved not having to search for the information again.

The local telephone directory has useful information that should be recorded. This list might include American Red Cross under Crisis Information; Visiting Nurse Association under Health Services; and items listed under Senior Citizens Services.

The yellow pages of your telephone directory will have information under headings such as Home Health Services, Nurses, Nursing Homes, Senior Citizen Service Organizations, and Social Service Organizations.

Large Crisis-Information Chart

Use a medium felt-tip, black pen to make a large crisis-information chart for aged parents. Print the letters and numbers at least an inch high for easy reading. List all numbers parents might need to call in a hurry. Arrange in alphabetical order: ambulance, doctor, electric company, gas company, hospital, plumber, police, yourself, other relatives.

In addition to the name and number, also print what should be said in case of an emergency. Example: "This is Elizabeth Benson. I live at 50 Oak Street. I need help." This will help individuals who may not handle a crisis easily. Valuable time will be saved. Keep a flashlight with charged batteries by the phone.

Nursing Skills

It will save time to learn some basic nursing skills. Consider a class in beginning nursing at a local community college. In most areas, the American Red Cross offers classes on basic skills for home care.

Home Healthcare

If your parents need medical care but do not require intensive care, life support systems, or any complicated treatment, you may be able to arrange for home healthcare. It is one of the oldest home care services in existence and is rapidly increasing in availability and popularity. Check with your parents' doctor for a recommendation.

Homemaking Services

If your parent-care responsibilities become overwhelming, you may want to consider a weekly homemaking service. Always check references before hiring anyone to come into your home.

Recording Memories

Set a specific time in your schedule for recording memories. This will bring strength to the family and help the older adult feel cherished and unique as personal achievements are shared.

Scripture says: *Remember the days of old; consider the generations long past. Ask your father and he will tell you, your elders, and they will explain to you* (Deut. 32:7).

A video recording of parents reflecting and reminiscing about the past will be meaningful. If they prefer to make a written life review, provide the necessary materials, such as a pencil and notebook, typewriter, or computer. Tape recordings of parents also can be transcribed at a later date.

Whatever form is chosen, encourage parents to include not only facts but also feelings about what they experienced. Capture memories from earliest childhood to the present. Anything that survives in their memory is significant. What a treasure this will be to future generations.

Ps. 78:4 says, *Tell the next generation the praiseworthy deeds of the Lord, his power, and the wonders he has done.* Include, in the chronicles, answers to prayer that parents remember. Then these mighty acts of God can be passed on from one generation to another.

"The family that writes together is a closer one," says Peter R. Stillman in *Families Writing* (Writer's Digest Books, 1989). He describes meaningful writing activities that can build links across generations, now and in the future.

Books-by-Mail Service

Some libraries offer a books-by-mail service. Books can be ordered from a catalog and returned in the same container, postage free.

Shopping by Mail

Time and money can be saved by purchasing items through a mail-order catalog. Before placing a mail order, check the guarantee and return policies. Never send cash through the mail. Photocopy the order form and your check before sending.

Priority Planner

It is easy for caregivers to feel overwhelmed as they view numerous areas of responsibility. Linda Dillow's *Priority Planner* (Nashville: Thomas Nelson, 1986) is a valuable tool for setting priorities, keeping a weekly and daily schedule, and keeping a shopping list.

Locating Help

Often caregivers cannot handle the demands of parent care without outside assistance. Fortunately, ample help is available.

Area Agency on Aging

The governor of each state designates area agencies on aging, which handle matters relating to the needs of the elderly in the community. These agencies provide information on local community resources available: home healthcare, home safety, repair programs, and personal care services.

Check the telephone directory under County Government for an Aging listing to locate the agency in your community. Or try the yellow pages under Senior Citizens.

American Association of Retired Persons

The best single source for help is AARP. If your parent is not a member, write for information: AARP, P.O. Box 199, Long Beach, CA 90801-9989.

Adult Day Care

Day care is a community-based program designed to meet the needs of frail or functionally impaired adults. It is a structured program providing a variety of health, social, and related support services during the day. Individuals who participate in adult day care attend on a planned basis during specified hours. This program helps participants remain in the community and enables families to continue caring for their loved one at home.

For a listing of adult day-care centers in your area or other publications on the subject write: The National Council on the Aging, 600 Maryland Ave. S.W., West Wing 100, Washington, DC 20024; or call toll-free 800-313-9046.

A new concept is intergenerational centers, where preschoolers and older adults are together. Children and elders do small-group activities together. Both age-groups naturally interact. This creative alternative is helpful for working caregivers.

Health Care Concepts

This Christian consulting company specializes in education and consultation to those caring for the older adult. Their services are personalized. They include private consultations, large-group seminars, and training sessions. Fees are very reasonable. For more information, contact them: 4006 Arsenal St., St. Louis, MO 63116 (314-773-7757).

Visiting Nurses Association

Visiting Nurses Association or other home healthcare organizations provide around-the-clock consultations, as well as hands-on care. This helps alleviate stress on all family members. These services are available in most communities.

Caregivers Practical Help

Such a wide range of problems can confront caregivers that special training to meet their needs is important for the well-being of both caregiver and care-receiver. The book *Caregivers Practical Help* provides how-to information and resources for those who provide informal care to their homebound elderly. For a copy write: Caregivers Practical Help, New York State Office for the Aging, P.O. Box 1041, Albany, NY 12220-2041.

Parent Care Publications

Parent Care Publications is a company offering services to the Christian caregiver. They review books on parent care and related topics. The most recommended titles are listed in their catalog and are in stock for fast shipment to you.

Parent Care is a monthly newsletter for children of aging parents. Included are realistic solutions to tough care-giving challenges; informative articles; new product information; useful tips and suggestions; inspirational thoughts; prayer needs; and experiences from other caregivers. For subscription information or a catalog, send a self-addressed, stamped envelope to: Parent Care, Box 216, Bethany, OK 73008.

Executive Director Betty Robertson is also available to conduct Parent Care seminars at local churches or speak at conferences. For further information, call 405-787-7272.

DISCUSSION QUESTIONS

1. Why is time so valuable?

2. How can we make the best use of our time as caregivers?

3. Do you feel pressured by time? If so, what practical steps can you take in your life to solve this problem?

4. What other gift ideas can you think of for older adults?

5. Which of the ideas under "Making Life Easier" would you like to put into practice this week?

— E I G H T —

Facing the Feelings

Love knows no limit to its endurance, no end to its trust, no fading of its hope; it can outlast anything. Love never fails. 1 COR. 13:7-8, PHILLIPS

Negative Collage

There is no way to know when the need to provide parent care will arrive. It may be while adult children still are struggling to bring up their own children or desperately trying to pay college bills. The adult child may be right at the peak of a career or already becoming an aging parent.

Then, when least expected, the problems of aging parents worm their way into a life—like tangled spaghetti. Soon a collage of negative feelings forms:

Anger—toward the parent who is ill or other family members who are free to pursue their own lives

Anguish—from being treated like a little child by the parents being attended

Anxiety—about the future, the finances, and the freedom lost

Apprehension—from looking at your parents and seeing yourself in the future

Chronic Grief—when daily caring for someone who is ill but will never recover

Confusion—of not knowing where, or to whom, to turn for help

Depression—because your life-style now seems so overwhelming

Fear—from wondering if a parent's illness will be inherited

Frustration—from trying to adequately care for elderly parents while continuing to meet the immediate family needs

Guilt—over thinking it would be easier to all involved if the parent just died

Helplessness—from seeing parent's health deteriorate

Impatience—in dealing with diet, disposition, and hygiene

Inadequacy—which overwhelms with a sob, "This responsibility is bigger than I am."

Irritation—because the water faucet is left running; and a favorite chair is soiled from incontinence

Isolation—from feeling no one REALLY understands

Pain—from remembering what it was like before a parent became "old"

Resentment—from encroachment on time and energy

Sadness—when the person you care about is aging at an accelerated rate

Stress—when all fibers of strength are taut

These feelings are normal. Sharing these emotions with a trusted friend is healthy. Dwelling on this negative composite, however, may lead to self-centeredness and bitterness.

Proper Perspective

In an era of instant everything, we want quick solutions to our problems. But God has a way of developing character qualities in our lives through the trials we face. *Suffering produces perseverance; perseverance, character,* Paul declares in Rom. 5:3-4.

When emotional conflicts surface, we have an opportunity to search for inner motives and attitudes. Experience and express the emotions. Then reflect, "God, what are You trying to teach me through this?"

Be willing to let God build some of the following character qualities in your life:

Availability—adjusting personal responsibilities around the needs of those whom you are serving

Contentment—realizing God has provided everything needed for present happiness

Endurance—inner strength to withstand stress

Flexibility—learning how to cheerfully change plans when unexpected conditions require it

Forgiveness—learning to demonstrate Christ's love toward an offender

Gentleness—learning to respond to needs with kindness and love

Patience—learning how to wait to fulfill personal goals. Learning to accept difficult situations as from God without giving Him a deadline to remove it.

Tolerance—viewing every person as a valuable individual whom God created and loves

Be patient. God will work these qualities in a willing heart. Paul was an old pro at handling difficulties. He wrote, *I haven't learned all I should even yet, but I keep working toward that day when I will finally be all that Christ saved me for and wants me to be. No, dear brothers, I am still not all I should be but I am bringing all my energies to bear on this one thing* (Phil. 3:12-13, TLB).

About This Thing Called Love

Love is very patient and kind, never jealous or envious, never boastful or proud, never haughty or selfish or rude.

Love does not demand its own way. It is not irritable or touchy.

It does not hold grudges and will hardly even notice when others do it wrong.

It is never glad about injustice, but rejoices whenever truth wins out.

If you love someone you will be loyal to him no matter what the cost.

You will always believe in him, always expect the best of him, and always stand your ground in defending him (1 Cor. 13:4-7, TLB).

God's kind of love says, "Even if I don't feel like it, I will do it—because it is right."

Think before reacting. The only person who can make you act in an unloving way is you. You determine the state of your emotions. There are two possible responses in interpersonal relationships: actions and reactions. We cannot control the actions of others; however, we can regulate our reactions.

If a bad attitude toward an aging parent surfaces, stop and think about your response. Are you treating your parent the way you would want to be treated? The Golden Rule still applies, *In everything, do to others what you would have them do to you* (Matt. 7:12).

Your name may be lost in the fog of age and medication, but the older adult cherishes your presence. Situations faced in caring for aging parents can be heartbreaking and soul-burdening. But we are reminded, *The greatest of these is love* (1 Cor. 13:13).

Family Meetings

Hold regular family meetings with all generations present. Air feelings, consider solutions to existing problems, exchange views, and handle complaints. Discuss difficult and sometimes explosive feelings. Communication is vital to a healthy, care-giving family.

Write remedial action on a chart and post for accountability purposes. This chart might read: Grandpa promises to rinse his whiskers down the sink after shaving; Grandma will work at saying one positive thing to every family member each day; Lucille will lower the volume on her stereo during the grandparents' nap time; Mother consents to letting Grandma cook one meal a week; Father agrees to putting a weekly date with Mom on his calendar.

Give positive feedback to one another at these meetings. Try one of these methods:

● **Bombardment**—choose one family member to bombard with positive comments. Speak directly to the individual: "Dad, I appreciate how sensitive you are to my feelings"; or "You are a wonderful son-in-law. I appreciate the spiritual leadership you give the family."

● **Here's My Heart**—If there are six people in the family, each person gets five white hearts, made from construction paper. Words of love and appreciation are written on the hearts, one message for each of the other family members. Hearts are then distributed.

● **Web of Love**—family members sit in a circle. The father has a ball of yarn. He wraps the yarn around his finger and then tosses the ball to someone. He expresses his appreciation to that person. This continues until a large "web" of love forms.

Close these sessions with a brief Bible study and prayer. The "'One Anothers' of Scripture" (Appendix, p. 99) are appropriate for this family time together. Choose one topic. Allow participation by family members through reading the scriptures, asking questions, or offering insights.

Col. 3:12-16 (TLB) has the solution for the feelings that arise when families care for aging parents. Read this passage often as a family:

Since you have been chosen by God who has given you this new kind of life, and because of his deep love and concern for you, you should practice tender-hearted mercy and kindness to others. Don't worry about making a good impression on them but be ready to suffer quietly and patiently. Be gentle and ready to forgive; never hold grudges. Remember, the Lord forgave you, so you must forgive others. Most of all, let love guide your life, for then the whole church will stay together in perfect harmony. Let the peace of heart which comes from Christ be always present in your hearts and lives, for this is your responsibility and privilege as members of his body. And always be thankful. Remember what Christ taught and let his words enrich your lives and make you wise; teach them to each other and sing them out in psalms and hymns and spiritual songs, singing to the Lord with thankful hearts.

DISCUSSION QUESTIONS

1. Which emotions are bottled up within you right now?

2. Which feeling has the most intensity?

3. What effects do negative emotions have upon you?

4. Which character quality will you prayerfully ask God to build into your life this week?

5. How does God want you to look at your situation?

6. What solutions are found in Col. 3:12-16 (TLB) for the feelings that arise in caring for aging parents?

───NINE───

Challenge of Coping

Don't you yet understand? Don't you know by now that the everlasting God, the Creator of the farthest parts of the earth, never grows faint or weary? No one can fathom the depths of his understanding. He gives power to the tired and worn out, and strength to the weak. Even the youths shall be exhausted, and the young men will all give up. But they that wait upon the Lord shall renew their strength. They shall mount up with wings like eagles; they shall run and not be weary; they shall walk and not faint.

ISA. 40:28-31, TLB

How do you cope as a caregiver? Get your eyes off the daily snapshots of difficult feelings. Focus instead on the big picture of fulfilling God's will. Working with God increases confidence and gives noble purpose to every aspect of care giving.

Constant joy is the result of living under the divine will rather than mere human will. *Moreover—let us be full of joy now! Let us exult and triumph in our troubles and rejoice in our sufferings, knowing that pressure and affliction and hardship produce patient and unswerving endurance. And endurance (fortitude) develops maturity of character* (Rom. 5:3-4, Amp.).

Daily Prayer

The most available resource for caregivers is prayer. *Do not be anxious about anything, but in everything, by prayer and petition, with thanksgiving, present your requests to God. And the peace of God, which transcends all understanding, will guard your hearts and your minds in Christ Jesus* (Phil. 4:6-7).

The establishment of personal, private time is crucial for your survival. Only God can whisper deep in your spirit. He can envelop us with peace and comfort in the midst of trauma. The Psalmist said, *My soul waits in silence for God only* (62:1, NASB).

You may query, "How can I establish a regular time with the Lord with all the hindrances that come by caring for an aging parent?" Examine the following tips by Millie Deitz, and discover it's easier than you think.

1. *Ask God to help you learn to pray.* Does this sound too simple? Think for a moment. If our children seek help from us, do we refuse them? Of course not. We are pleased when they ask, and we even feel closer to

them. In the same manner, God wants your companionship, and He will help you.

2. *Set five minutes aside each day to pray.* None of us would neglect to brush our hair or wash our faces daily, claiming, "There just wasn't time." Don't we always make time for these necessities? Then let's make it a daily choice to spend five minutes with God. If at all possible, try to schedule it at the same time and place for a whole week.

3. *Pray aloud.* At first this may seem peculiar, to talk with no one around. But our thoughts dart so rapidly, it becomes difficult to remain focused in prayer. Haven't you noticed how often your mind wanders during prayers? One way to concentrate on a spirit of prayer is to take the time to put each thought into words.

4. *Start a prayer list.* Be specific in what you ask God to do. Write down exactly what you asked and when. This will help you know how and when your prayers are answered. Some prayers are granted immediately. Others take longer. Keeping a record will both prevent you from forgetting and give proof of His answers. (See Appendix, p. 101, "Prayer Requests.")

5. *Use short prayers throughout the day.* Some have referred to these as "bullet prayers." If a particular situation or person flashes through your mind, immediately target in and say a short prayer.

Praying the Scriptures is a way of using portions of the Bible as a framework in communicating with God. Some verses already are personalized, and others need to be paraphrased. The Psalms lend themselves to this. Pat Rulo shares an example of personalizing Phil. 4:13, 19:

"O Father in heaven, Your Word tells me that I can do all things through You and that You will give Me the strength needed and that You will meet all of my needs according to Your glorious riches in Christ Jesus."

Prayerlife Ministries offers 10 *Prayer Break* devotional tapes with prayer times. Glaphré Gilliland shares the comfort, challenge, and practical guidance of God's Word in reachable steps. These tapes include: "When the Pieces Don't Fit"; "I Need to Depend on God"; "Jesus Heals Our Hurts, Our Scrapes," and "Climbing Out of Your Box." Write to: Prayerlife, Bethany, OK 73008.

Glaphré is also author of *Talking with God: A Woman's Workshop on Prayer* (Beacon Hill Press of Kansas City).

Daily Bible Reading

Reading the Bible is *useful to teach us what is true and to make us realize what is wrong in our lives; it straightens us out and helps us do what is right. It is God's way of making us well prepared at every point, fully equipped to do good to everyone* (2 Tim. 3:16-17, TLB).

Paul's testimony was, *This is the reason why we never lose heart. The outward man does indeed suffer wear and tear, but every day the inward man receives fresh strength* (2 Cor. 4:16, Phillips).

Deliberately focus your mind on the selected daily scripture. Examine each word or phrase until its depth captures you. Allow the power of the Holy Spirit to transform your life.

For consistent, daily reading of God's Word, a plan should be followed:

● Some caregivers have found that the Psalms precisely speak to their experiences. This Bible book can be completed in a month by reading a given number of Psalms a day. One method is to read every 30th psalm: Day 1—Psalms 1, 31, 61, 91, 121; Day 2—Psalms 2, 32, 62, 92, 122; Day 3—Psalms 3, 33, 63, 93, 123; etc.

● Many daily decisions and unique situations face adult children who care for their parents. The wisdom of God can be gained by reading one chapter of Proverbs each day. There are 31 chapters. The book was written *to teach . . . people how to live—how to act in every circumstance* (Prov. 1:2, TLB).

● Read a portion of Scripture until it is internalized. An entire month could be spent studying the specific commands of God given in James. Extended time could be given to such passages as 1 Corinthians 13 and Psalm 119.

● *The One-Year Bible* is arranged in 365 daily selections that make reading through the Bible enjoyable.

Scripture Memorization

Ps. 119:11 (TLB) says, *I have thought much about your words, and stored them in my heart.* Regular intake of spiritual food is vital. Digestion comes through memorizing scripture. When God's Word is in your heart and mind, it becomes active within you.

What area of need are you facing? Find a related verse. Write it on a self-stick removable note pad sheet or 3" x 5" card. Memorize the verse while blow-drying your hair, washing dishes, ironing, standing in the supermarket checkout line, walking, or waiting for a green traffic light.

Focus on Positive Aspects

Intermittent negative feelings are normal. How easy it is to focus on the negative. It takes effort to concentrate on the positive aspects of caring.

Mother's dementia became gradually worse. She became incontinent and had no bowel control. The first few times I had to clean her stool, I was angry, resentful, and feeling sorry for myself. I kept thinking, Why me? I avoided looking at Mother. But one time I saw her pain-filled eyes and realized that even though she could not express her feelings, she was humiliated. I had been so concerned about my own discomfort, I had not stopped to think about hers. I asked God to forgive me and help me think positively.

There will be many irritations. Pray for an inner quietness in spite of outward irritations: *the peace of God, which transcends all understanding* (Phil. 4:7). A relationship with aging parents cannot endure without forbearance and flexibility. Give the benefit of the doubt.

The best survival technique is learning how to cope with new responsibilities. Don't fight them. Accept the fact of generations together. Understand there will be problems. Your performance may not be perfect, but you can do your best.

Prayer Partner

Find someone who will commit to pray for you daily. Scripture says, *Two are better than one, because they have a good return for their work: If one falls down, his friend can help him up. But pity the man who falls and has no one to help him up!* (Eccles. 4:9-10).

Accepting Help

God will give strength for the work He plans for you, but not for the work He plans for others to do. Accept offers of help from family and friends. People usually will not volunteer unless they really want to help. This outside diversion from your normal activities will be refreshing.

Plan for complete periodic breaks from care giving. This should not be a desperate effort to escape, but a planned change of pace—a respite, a much-deserved retreat.

Respite care offers a temporary relief service to give caregivers a break. These programs can be run in the home or on a residential basis at a hospital or nursing home. Unfortunately, there is no national organization to contact about respite care. Normally a physician or a hospital social worker can give resource information. Ask a friend, neighbor, or fellow parishioner to "parent sit" for an afternoon.

Daily Journal

Keep a daily journal of your somersaulting feelings. Writing may prove to be a vital release of feelings. It helps clarify relationships. Surprisingly, writing a journal sometimes is more helpful than talking to a friend. A journal never gives advice. It just listens.

A journal can be told things that could not be said to anyone. Express the turmoil or joys of life. Write whatever comes to mind. Air the frustrations, fears, and wishes. It brings release, insight, and understanding. No one should ever read a personal journal unless asked. These are your feelings.

Support Group

Shirley Posey teaches a large Sunday School class of adults, ages 30 to 50. She started a support group from the class for children with aging parents to meet a deep-felt need. The group meets once a week in her home. They have 8 to 12 in attendance.

The format for each meeting is prayer and general conversation. The one under the most stress begins the discussion. This person often is in a crisis situation and needs to talk about feelings. The group listens to and supports each other while sharing experiences. They cry together. Some of the wounds of care giving are healed by laughing together.

"While the instigation of this group was spontaneous, my prayer is that everything that is said and done will be of the Lord, not just a human answer," said Shirley. "I certainly do not want to mislead or hurt any of these friends in their walks with God. My intent is to *support* them in their times of need."

Group members offer suggestions to one another of things that worked for them in certain situations. They also invite professionals to speak, such as a psychologist, geriatric nurse, or senior-adult pastor.

Support groups are helpful for networking with people who have similar experiences. If the home church does not have a support group for adult children of aging parents, consider organizing one.

How to Organize a Support Group

1. Determine the objective with a brief statement summarizing the purpose of the group. The definition of a supportive fellowship can be found in Gal. 6:2, 9-10.

2. Obtain permission from the pastor.

3. Put the following notice in your church bulletin and newsletter: "A support group is beginning for adult children caring for aging parents. If you would like to participate, please come to the organizational meeting (date and time)."

4. Personally invite any potential caregivers.

5. At the organizational session, state the objective. Set a regular date, time, and place for meetings.

6. Determine a format for the regular meetings, perhaps based on this example:

   a. Open with prayer.

   b. Introduce any new attendees with a warm welcome.

   c. Choose a question to springboard discussion; e.g., What is the one thing that overwhelms you the most as a caregiver?

   d. Elicit personal responses.

   e. Pray for one another, based on the burdens shared during discussion.

   f. Share a truth from God's Word. Scripture should play a central role in the support group. *Focus on God's Word* is a collection of Bible studies designed for adult children caring for aging parents. Write Parent Care, P.O. Box 216, Bethany, OK 73008, for information (enclose SASE).

   g. Choose one person to bombard with affirmation.

   h. Give practical ideas, such as those found in this book.

   i. Occasionally invite special speakers.

   j. Close with a song, testimony, or prayer.

7. At the first session, become acquainted with each other so that honest discussion and interaction can take place.

8. This can be an outreach for your church. Encourage participants to invite friends, neighbors and co-workers who also are caregivers.

A daughter providing parent care shared, "The first thing Mother says to me every day is, 'I wish I could die.' I'm losing her day by day. When my responsibilities overwhelm me, I turn to my support group. After a meeting, the load seems easier."

Laugh

Use the "flipside technique." Turn the problems you are having with your aging parents over and find humor in the situation. This will help you survive.

The gift of laughter makes life easier. Jane Brody, a highly regarded writer on health matters, says it is vital to "use the uniquely human expression of mirth to reduce stress, ease pain, and generally brighten one's outlook on life, regardless of how grim the reality."

Solomon said it this way: *A cheerful heart is good medicine* (Prov. 17:22). A hearty laugh can relax taut nerves and ease weariness.

Keep on the lookout for humorous happenings, statements, and one-liners. Share these with your family. Take a few moments to watch the Pink Panther on a videocassette, listen to Bill Cosby on an audiocassette, or read an Erma Bombeck book. Check out collections of humor from your library.

If laughter is the best medicine, you'll want to read a dose of *You're Only Old Once!* by Dr. Seuss (Random House). Eighty-two-year-old Ted Geisel wrote this wonderful spoof on the trials and tribulations of growing older. You will relate easily to these trials.

Dotsey Welliver, in her book *Laughing Together* (Brethren Press), says: "Laughter is God's gift. It is vital to our welfare. It can help us through the barren deserts in life. A humorous perspective can lighten the load of our daily work and help us transcend some of our trials."

Exercise

TAKE CARE OF YOURSELF! Maintain a regular exercise program. Exercise briskly at least 15-30 minutes three times a week. When combined with good eating habits, potential exercise benefits include increased stamina and strength; more restful sleep; greater resistance to stress, anxiety, and fatigue; a more radiant appearance; improved mental health; and reduced risk of illness.

Working at Home

The adult child who is homebound because of parent care may want to consider the varied possibilities of working at home. Many businesses can be operated from home: day care, music lessons, tutoring, upholstering, cooking and selling specialty food items, writing, bookkeeping service, plant sitter, wake-up service, creating and marketing handcrafted items, custom sewing, beauty consultant, income tax preparation, refinishing furniture, and parties for selling products—to name a few.

An increasing number of women are jumping off the career track to raise families or care for aging parents or both. Home businesses can be a creative outlet and bolster income.

Define an area of interest. Learn all you can by reading about that field. Check local zoning requirements and tax guidelines. Do not overextend financially. Be wary of get-rich-quick schemes. If it sounds too good to be true, it probably is! The greatest advertising always has been by word of mouth.

Check the library for two helpful books: *Home Business Resource Guide,* by Cheryl Gorder (Blue Bird Publishing), and *The Work-at-Home Sourcebook,* by Lynie Arden (Live Oak Publications, 6003 N. 51st St., No. 105, P.O. Box 2193, Boulder, CO 80306).

Sandwich Generation Resources

If you are sandwiched between caring for aging parents and caring for your own children, there are helpful resources. *365 TV-Free Activities You Can Do with Your Child,* by Steve and Ruth Bennet (Bob Adams, 1991) provides games and activities that require little or no preparation, yet provide hours of entertainment and play. *52 Simple Ways to Have Fun with Your Child,* by Carl Dreizler (Thomas Nelson Publishers, 1991), is useful for parents and grandparents in setting up regular times to have fun with the kids.

DISCUSSION QUESTIONS

1. Why is a daily devotional time with God so vital?

2. How would you rate your daily prayer life now?

3. Which Bible reading idea would you like to try?

4. Which of the following scriptures will you choose to memorize this week? 1 Chron. 28:20; Pss. 55:22; 121:1-2; Isa. 40:31; 43:2; 1 Cor. 13:4-5; James 1:2-4.

5. Why is it important to focus on the positive aspects of care giving?

TEN

Dealing with Death

May the Lord of peace himself give you his peace no matter what happens. 2 THESS. 3:16, TLB

Being Realistic

I plodded into the house after attending a day-long business meeting. Daddy's light was still on. We chatted briefly. Then he hurled a word grenade that exploded my heart and shattered my composure: "Mother and I said our final farewells today. You never know when one of us is going to pass away. Some people die in their sleep. Others just go. So we got that out of the way." Every corpuscle of my being screamed, "Please don't ever leave me." I know all of life is made of seasons, but the harsh, unrelenting winter was coming—sooner than I had expected.

I learned in kindergarten that all living things eventually die. Death is unwelcome. We would all like to hold it in abeyance. Accepting the reality of our parents' death is painful. It makes us confront our own mortality.

The elderly grasp the certainty of death more readily than the young. It's their adult children who usually change the subject or dismiss it. We want to slow the endless ticking of the clock of mortality. We are uncomfortable facing the fact our parents will die someday. Our line with the past will be broken—beyond repair. And when a parent dies, there is no escaping the reality: our generation is next in line.

For many, life without parents is unthinkable. Often the presence of parents is taken for granted until they become older or ill. Then reality hits with hurricane force. They will not be around forever. At some point, the mortality of older adults must be accepted.

Our children also need to be prepared for their grandparents' death. When equipped with the right information, children usually can handle crises. Children under age two will only sense that something is wrong. They will need extra attention and love. Through age five, boys and girls will not understand, and they will have questions. Older children need to know what is expected.

Fear of death is the most universal anxiety of life. Use a family time together to discuss what death is; feelings about it; and life after death.

Discussion Starters for Family Time

- What is the inevitable end of the earthly life cycle?
  Death. Heb. 9:27 says, *Man is destined to die once, and after that to face judgment.* Death is not the end of human existence. See 1 Corinthians 15.

- Was death a part of God's original creation?
  Read Gen. 3:19. It only became "natural" after mankind's sin.
- If you had a choice, how would you want to die?
- What is the difference between death and dying?
- Which do you fear most and why?
- What do you want to accomplish before dying?
- How did Jesus feel about His own death?
  Read Matt. 26:36-39 and Heb. 5:7.
- What is the assurance Jesus gives to those who have accepted Him as personal Savior?
  Read John 3:16.
- Is death the end of life?

Death is seen as final, and endings are painful. Leaving the known for the unknown is not easy. But through the resurrection of Jesus Christ, death has been transformed from an ending to a beginning. Read John 11:25-26.

Scriptures to Read About Life After Death

John 14:1-6	Christ's revelation of heaven
Revelation 21	Description of heaven
Revelation 4	A scene in heaven
Luke 20:27-38	What life in heaven is like
1 Kings 8:30	God's dwelling place
Job 3:17	Place of rest for saints
Ps. 16:11	Place of fullness of joy
2 Cor. 5:1	An everlasting abode of saints

Field Trip

Call a local funeral home and ask if your family could tour the facilities. Explain that you want your children to see a mortuary so that they are not scared when a grandparent dies and is taken to one.

Planning Ahead

Facing death realistically makes necessary planning easier. Every few months Daddy would say, "Whenever you have time, please bring me the files labeled 'Important Papers' and 'Funeral Arrangements.'" After examining all the items, he would go over it all with me again. My outward response was a smile and "OK." Inwardly my heart yelled, "I don't want to talk about it." But Daddy's detailed planning decreased the responsibility my husband, my brothers, and I faced.

Complete the "Funeral Planning Form" for both your parents (Appendix, pp. 83-86). Fill in all blank spaces as soon as possible. Working on this now will eliminate unnecessary problems later. Planning facilitates arrangements.

This organizing also personalizes the funeral. The message, words of remembrance, and style should fit parents and conform to their wishes.

Requested Measures of Care

Be aware of terms used by the medical profession:
- Life Support—Anything that keeps life going.

- Extraordinary Measure—Beyond what is ordinary to maintain life.
- Comfort Care—No procedures or treatments are to be done for diagnostic reasons.
- No Code—No resuscitative measures are to be taken.

All professionals caring for elderly parents should be apprised of their wishes. Have available copies of living wills (see chapter 6). Be sure correct information is written on all medical records.

A "No Code" sign can be placed as a reminder to emergency technicians, as well as physicians. "Comfort Care Only" should be posted also so that no procedures or treatments are done for diagnostic reasons, but only to alleviate discomfort.

How to Recognize Death

While Daddy was alive, the morning ritual was unchanged. He awakened before Mother and waited for help out of bed. I tiptoed in, opened the blind, and waited for him to say, "Good morning." I knew if he talked to me, he was still alive! With no previous experience with death, I didn't know what to expect.

How does one recognize death?
- Eyes are fixed.
- Heartbeat and breathing stop.
- Mouth may be open and motionless.
- Skin turns pale (perhaps blue) and cold.
- After 30 to 60 minutes, extremities become stiff.

Steps to Take

Procedures to follow vary from state to state when someone dies. Ask the funeral home you plan to use for requirements of state laws. Talk with all family members about the steps that need to be taken. Post the information.

Facing Death in the Hospital

If a parent has only a short time to live and must be hospitalized, talk with the physician about a private room. The final hours should be a family time. Privacy is imperative. Hospitals often allow family members the privilege of round-the-clock time in the room with the patient.

If a "no extraordinary measure" decision has been made, be positive a "No Code" is posted plainly on all records.

Politely request items needed to make your vigilant stay comfortable. A cot, extra chairs, pillows, and blankets are useful.

Facing Death at Home

A dying parent may choose the comfort of home. Theologian Francis Schaeffer was dying of cancer. He appealed to be taken home, surrounded by familiar things and people he loved.

Rather than staring at green hospital walls, Dr. Schaeffer gazed out four large glass panels, enjoying the trees with their first spring leaves.

On a continuing basis, the family played his favorite records. He was listening to Handel's *Messiah* when he exhaled his last earthly breath.

Hospice

Hospice care means providing comfort and reassurance to the dying in a peaceful setting. Hospice is an old concept that has had a growing acceptance, with 1,700 programs now available across the country. It's an alternative to aggressive, sometimes excessive, medical treatment. John Bailey says, "One of the great values of the hospice experience is the way it brings the family together and teaches each member to value life" (*Parent Care* newsletter, May 1992).

Hospice nurses strive to alleviate pain and reassure fears. Services are provided in special buildings, separate hospital wings, or in the home.

Under terms of the Catastrophic Coverage Act, Medicare now provides coverage for these services in a Medicare-certified hospice, with certain limitations. These will need to be clarified and documented by your physician and insurance carrier.

For the nearest hospice address, call a local hospital or contact: National Hospice Organization, 1901 N. Moore St., Suite 901, Arlington, VA 22209 (toll-free 800-658-8895). Two free brochures, *The Basics of Hospice* and *About Hospice,* are available from this organization.

When It's Time to Say Good-bye

Jacob's last days are recorded in Genesis 47—50. Knowing death was imminent, he called for the sons, grandsons, and their families. Jacob conferred a blessing. This was his spiritual will—his time of summing up and sorting out, passing on the heritage to future generations.

You may want to have Communion together one final time. If so, contact your pastor. What a joy to break bread and drink the cup in the fellowship of the family.

Confirm your love. If your family is not accustomed to openly showing emotions, take the initiative to tell your parent, "I love you." Eliminate at least one of the "I wish I would haves."

Daddies Don't Die

I was concerned when Daddy said, "I wanted to see the performance you're directing tonight, but I'm just too weak." Being his primary caregiver for two years, I had learned to cope with many uncertainties surrounding Parkinson's disease. This was one of them.

Later in the day, he registered a fever, and his breathing became labored. My husband took him to the emergency room for an examination. I fulfilled my responsibilities for the evening, fully expecting Daddy to be in his bed when I returned home.

My husband returned from the hospital alone. He explained that Daddy had contracted pneumonia and was in intensive care. For some reason, I did not equate intensive care with serious. Sure, he was 83, but he had survived several serious operations. I was confident he would soon be back in his favorite chair in the sitting room.

Three days later, my mind desperately tried to comprehend the words: "fatal" . . . "little chance" . . . "he has three to five days to live." My face crumpled under the devastating blow. Sobs gushed from the bottom of this daughter's heart. I wept with all the anguish of one whose joy had permanently fled.

My entire life structure rocked with a whirlwind of suffering. Everything in me screamed denial. I wanted to yell, "NO! DADDIES DON'T DIE!"

I dried the scalding tears. Then, stepping to his side, I whispered, "Daddy, I'm going to miss you. I love you so much."

He replied, "It's hard to say good-bye."

The writer in me determined to record everything he said from that moment. Conversations were jotted on paper towels, magazine ads, and scraps of paper.

During his lifetime, my father had traveled 1½ million miles in his line of work. With white-knuckled determination, I vowed we would make this last journey together. The hospital provided a private room. My purpose was to help Daddy die comfortably and with dignity. At times, I felt strangled by the antiseptic smells, the maze of tubes, the foreboding mask, the thumping noise of the monitoring machine. But I seldom left his side.

His final words were, "I have never felt so tired." Between morphine injections, I would rub sore muscles, offer cold water, and whisper, "Daddy, I love you" . . . "I'm so proud of you" . . . "You can go now. It's OK."

And then, at 11:15 P.M. on a Wednesday evening, I discovered daddies do die. For 45 years, he had been a living presence in my life. Now . . . a memory of love.

Letting Go

Before Daddy died, I had been hand-holding with a friend whose father was terminally ill. One day the phone rang. There were convulsive sobs. Phyllis whispered, "He's gone."

After verbally soothing her ravaging pain, I mailed this note: "That diseased, misshapen, hurting body is gone. The memories, godly inheritance, hope of seeing him again are yours forever. You have no regrets, no misgivings, no 'if onlys.' The heart pain is excruciating; your sense of loss is unbearable. But he'll always be your daddy. Not even death can snatch that away."

A line in Robert Anderson's play, *I Never Sang for My Father*, says: "Death ends a life . . . but it does not end a relationship." If the whirling carousel of grief would decelerate, the reality of those 11 words could be grasped. The letting-go process can be the primary caregiver's Mount Everest. Because of the daily involvement and interaction, emotions are deep. My letting go was not a major stage production, but rather a short monologue. "Jesus," I whispered, "You'll have to take care of Daddy now." And with a deliberate decision of my will, I let Him become the sole Caregiver.

Guilt can ride piggyback at this juncture. No matter what you did for your elderly parent, you may believe it was not enough. Accept the fact you did your best. Relinquish residual feelings to God. *Let not your heart be troubled* (John 14:1, KJV).

What Now?

After a parent dies, your pastor can walk you through the necessary procedure. Have available your "Funeral Planning Form" (Appendix, p. 83).

If extended family members need to make airline reservations, have them inquire about bereavement fares. Many companies realize funerals leave families no time to make advance purchases, and will waive restrictions.

If a funeral home field trip was not taken, talk with your children about what can be expected. Describe the room where the casket will be, what people do when they pay respects, why all the flowers are there, and how long the child needs to stay.

Younger children need to know their grandparent is lying down in a box called a casket. Explain they will look basically the same but will be lying still, with their eyes closed.

Show them the bottom half of the body is there. It is customary to open the casket only halfway.

Never pressure a child to do anything he would rather not, such as touching the body. My children were teenagers when Daddy died. They had never seen a corpse before. It seemed unreal to them when it happened. Curiosity prompted the question, "Is it OK to touch Grandpa?" They both wanted to discover what death "felt" like. Their response: "It's cold . . . it's hard . . . it's reality."

Children should not be forced to go to the funeral home or the funeral. If they would rather not attend the service, encourage them to express why. They may prefer to live with memories of their loved one. Some parents find a "good-bye gift" helps children realize the finality of death. This may mean helping to pick out the flowers, selecting music for the funeral, or making a special gift to put in the casket.

Closure

For many, death's finality comes at the cemetery. For me, it came at the final memorial service, when I knew the coffin lid would soon be closed. Never again would I see that beloved face I had called "Daddy" for 45 years.

I stood by the casket with tears cascading down my cheeks. My husband gently pulled at my left arm. Everyone was patiently waiting to start the cemetery trip. I could not move.

My head told me, "This is just his outer form." Attachment caused me to linger by the body that housed my daddy's substance. I finally leaned over and kissed him one last time. My heart cried, "Good-bye, Daddy. I love you." Then, resolutely, I departed.

Give Yourself Time

"Death holds no fear for the Christian" is a familiar phrase. Theory articulation is easier than living the belief. I always believed in heaven.

But until I hand-held with Daddy through his crossing of worlds, I was apprehensive about death. I had never been around it. The unknown can be frightening. But as I watched Daddy slip from this life into the next, I realized death is simply a transition.

The morning after Daddy died, I was Raggedy Ann limp. I lumbered into the dining room. My husband and brothers paused in their conversation to say, "Good morning." My mouth opened to reply, but only an inadvertent sob of grief escaped. My big brother responded, "Sis, it's OK. Daddy's in heaven now—with a body free from the effects of Parkinson's disease." I acknowledged his reminder of immortal hope with a nod.

My heart, however, did not feel this message of triumph. Drawn-out months passed before I—the little sis, the only daughter—felt the joy of resurrection. Then the psalm I memorized during childhood became a reality in my life: *Yea, though I walk through the valley of the shadow of death, I will fear no evil: for thou art with me; thy rod and thy staff they comfort me* (23:4, KJV).

Life Goes On

A cut finger hurts until the healing process is complete. A scab forms. Then finally a scar is all that remains. Grief is the deepest wound possible. Like a cut finger, healing occurs in stages. It leaves a scar.

The Adult Child and Family Deal with Grief

Grief recovery is a process:

1. Accept the reality of the loss.
2. Deal with feelings:
   Anger—"Why?"
   Guilt—"If only . . ."
   Sadness—"What will I do now?"
   Relief—after extended care giving
3. Accept the physical and mental pain of grieving.
4. Believe you will eventually reach a point where you can creatively continue your life.

The Surviving Parent

You may have a dual burden: dealing with your loss and being sensitive to the surviving parent's grief. One sympathy card noted: "I'm especially praying for your mother, who now has as much of her heart in heaven as she does on this earth." Matt. 19:5 tells of a man uniting to his wife and the two becoming one. The remaining spouse is now one-half a person.

Your surviving parent will need time to mourn and sort through the confusion of being alone. This disruption to a stable life-style must be handled gently. Spend time with the surviving spouse. Allow release of feelings. For one caregiver, it was a Mother's Day, 15 months after her father's death, before she realized she was expecting her mother to fill the gap left by her father's death. The unrealistic expectations she had of her mother hindered the grieving process for both.

Grieving has no specific time limit. It is a process. Studies on grief such as those by Elisabeth Kübler Ross in her book *On Death and Dying* show phases that may be experienced:

Denial—protective device that allows for slow acceptance.

Numbness—devoid of feeling.

Disorganization and forgetfulness—this phase may come and go.

Anger—at a loved one leaving.

Guilt—over things you neglected to do.

Depression—is normal and usually passes with time.

Acceptance—willingness to create a new life-style.

Awareness of grief stages can bring comfort in knowing your experience is not unique.

Watch for these normal responses to grief:

1. Change in sleep patterns
2. Apathy—lack of emotion or interest in life
3. Energy decline
4. Loss of appetite
5. Health and personal hygiene deterioration
6. Feeling of hopelessness
7. Dwelling on the past
8. Hibernation—withdrawing from normal activities

Help your parent make the transition from married to widowed life. Encourage:

- The finding of a bereavement companion who can lend a sympathetic ear and give additional support
- Additional healthcare of eating balanced meals and taking vitamins if nutritional supplement is needed
- Creative routines, different from what the couple experienced together
- Keeping in touch with old friends
- An activity while eating, such as listening to music, watching television, or reading a book
- Keeping active
- Ministry to others, looking beyond self to needs

DISCUSSION QUESTIONS

1. What does the Bible tell us about life after death?
2. Why is saying good-bye emotionally as well as verbally a crucial part of grieving?
3. How do people deny the death of a loved one?
4. What can be done to help a surviving parent deal with the loss of a spouse?

AFTERWORD

You have just completed reading *TLC for Aging Parents.* If I can be of any further help, I would enjoy hearing from you.

Have you subscribed to *Parent Care,* a monthly newsletter for children of aging parents? The purpose of the newsletter is to inform, encourage, and unite. Readers not only receive regular support but also are invited to take an active part in sharing their experiences with others. Each issue contains informative articles, useful tips and suggestions, response to questions, prayer needs, book reviews, new product information, inspiration from God's Word, and experiences from other children caring for aging parents.

Do you need a catalog of parent care books and resources? I review books on caring for aging parents and keep many in stock for fast shipment to you.

Would your church be interested in hosting a parent care seminar or conference? Contact me for further information.

Are you overwhelmed by your care-giving responsibilities? Parent Care has a group of prayer partners. Feel free to send your name and need.

When corresponding, please send a legal-size, self-addressed, stamped envelope for my reply to you.

Betty B. Robertson, Executive Director
Parent Care
P.O. Box 216
Bethany, OK 73008

APPENDIX

For your convenience, supplemental material has been cross-referenced. You may reproduce any material in this appendix for your personal use.

	Chapter(s)	Page(s)
Daily Care Plan	7	81
Funeral Planning Form	7, 10	83
Health Insurance Record	6	87
Home Safety Checklist	5	89
Medical History Chart	7	91
Medicine Chart	7	93
Monthly Meal Planner	7	95
Nursing Home Checklist	5	97
"One Anothers" of Scripture	8	99
Prayer Requests	9	101

Daily Care Plan

Normal wake-up time: _____

Assistive devices needed: ☐ glasses; ☐ hearing aid; ☐ dentures; ☐ cane; ☐ walker

Bath time: _____ Procedure: _____

_____

Eating times: Breakfast _____ Lunch _____ Dinner _____

     P.M. Snack _____

Any special eating difficulties:

     ☐ Needs assistance   ☐ Difficulty chewing   ☐ Difficulty swallowing

     ☐ Special utensils used: _____

Exercise time: _____ Routine: _____

_____

Toileting routine/schedule: _____

_____

Times/channels of favorite TV programs:

_____ _____

_____ _____

_____ _____

Times/stations of favorite radio programs:

_____ _____

_____ _____

_____ _____

If bedfast, times to rotate positions:

_____ left side _____ back _____ right side _____ up in chair

_____ left side _____ back _____ right side _____ up in chair

Usual bedtime: _____ Preferred amount of covers: _____ _____

_____

Preferred night clothes: _____

Time/dosage of medications:

Name	Dosage	Time(s)
_____	_____	_____
_____	_____	_____
_____	_____	_____
_____	_____	_____

Funeral Planning Form

Full legal name: _____

Social Security number: _____

Legal residence: _____

Place of birth: _____ Date: _____

Father's name: _____

Place of birth: _____ Date: _____

Mother's maiden Name: _____

Place of birth: _____ Date: _____

Educational degree: _____ Institution: _____

Educational degree: _____ Institution: _____

Educational degree: _____ Institution: _____

Name of spouse: _____

Place of marriage: _____ Date: _____

Names of children:

_____ Birth date: _____

_____ Birth date: _____

_____ Birth date: _____

_____ Birth date: _____

_____ Birth date: _____

Employers:

_____ Date of employment: _____

_____ Date of employment: _____

_____ Date of employment: _____

_____ Date of employment: _____

Awards: _____

_____

Veteran: ☐ Yes ☐ No Which war? _____

Date enlisted: _____ Branch of service: _____

Discharge date: _____ Serial no.: _____

Location of discharge papers: _____

Honors: _____

Location of will or trust: _____

Safe-deposit box no.: _____ Located at: _____

Location of safe-deposit key: _____

Checking acct. no.: _____ Institution: _____

Address: _____ Phone: _____

Savings acct. no.: _____ Institution: _____

Address: _____ Phone: _____

Savings acct. no.: _____ Institution: _____

Address: _____ Phone: _____

Credit card name: _____ Number: _____

Credit card name: _____ Number: _____

Credit card name: _____ Number: _____

Credit card name: _____ Number: _____

Religious affiliation: _____

Minister's name/phone: _____

Address: _____

Lawyer's name/phone: _____

Address: _____

Executor of estate/phone: _____

Address: _____

Medicare number: _____

Medicaid number: _____

Insurance Policies: _____

Company	Address	Phone	Policy Number	Face Amount

If funeral expenses have been prepaid:

Plan or policy number: _____

Name/phone of company: _____

Address: _____

Location of information: _____

If funeral expenses have not been prepaid:

Suggested name of funeral home: _____

Phone: _____ Address: _____

Buried or entombed at what cemetery: _____

Location: _____

Own space or crypt number? _____

What type of service?

☐ Memorial service without body present

☐ Service with body present and everyone welcome to attend

☐ Service with body present and only close family and friends attending

Service to take place at: _____

Address:_____ Phone: _____

Suggestions of person to officiate:

_____ Phone: _____

_____ Phone: _____

Suggestions for musicians:

_____ Phone: _____

_____ Phone: _____

Suggestions of person to read eulogy:

_____ Phone: _____

_____ Phone: _____

To be included in the service:

Music: _____

_____

_____

Scripture: _____

_____

_____

Other: _____

_____

_____

Suggestions for pallbearers:

_____	Phone: _____
_____	Phone: _____
_____	Phone: _____
_____	Phone: _____
_____	Phone: _____
_____	Phone: _____
_____	Phone: _____
_____	Phone: _____

Casket:

☐ to be open for viewing before the service   ☐ to be open during the service

☐ to be open only for close family and friends   ☐ to be closed at all times

Kind and color of flowers for casket:

_____

Memorial gift to be sent in my memory to:

_____

_____

_____

_____

Relatives and friends to contact:

Relationship	Name	Phone
_____	_____	_____
_____	_____	_____
_____	_____	_____
_____	_____	_____
_____	_____	_____
_____	_____	_____
_____	_____	_____
_____	_____	_____
_____	_____	_____
_____	_____	_____
_____	_____	_____
_____	_____	_____

Health Insurance Record

Date	Service Rendered	Amount Charged	Amt. Billed Medicare	Amt. Submitted Supplemental	Amt. Paid Medicare	Amt. Paid Supplemental	Amt. Not Reimbursed That You Paid

Home Safety Checklist

☐ Working smoke detector on every floor, including one near parent's room

☐ Well-secured handrails on both sides of all stairs, inside and out

☐ Light switches at both bottom and top of stairs

☐ Steps marked that are especially narrow or have risers that are higher or lower than the others

☐ Edges of outdoor steps painted white to be seen better at night

☐ All objects removed from stairways

☐ Carpet firmly attached to steps all along stairs

☐ Adequate lighting on all stairs, inside and out, so that each step, particularly the step edges, can be clearly seen

☐ Rough-surfaced adhesive strips in bathtub

☐ Well-secured towel racks

☐ Nonslip bath mat (preferably wall-to-wall carpeting)

☐ Two nonbreakable grab bars in bathtubs and showers (one attached to structural supports in the wall and one attached to side of tub)

☐ Hair dryers, shavers, and curling irons unplugged when not in use

☐ Hot and cold taps labeled

☐ Hot-water heater turned below 120 degrees to prevent burns

☐ Plastic drinking glasses

☐ Heavy pots and pans kept on lower shelves

☐ Safety caps on all household cleaning agents

☐ Night-lights in bedroom and bathroom

☐ Lamps or switches located close to each bed (rearrange furniture if necessary)

☐ Furniture arranged to decrease obstacles

☐ Abrasive material such as sand added to porch paint to help prevent slipping on smooth surface or ice

☐ "Tripping hazards" removed:

    ☐ Scatter rugs, runners, and mats

    ☐ Threshold stripping

    ☐ Electric cords and telephone wires

    ☐ Carpet tacked down or apply double-faced adhesive tape

Remember to recheck your home every year.

Medical History Chart

Name: _____

Mother's maiden name: _____

Date of birth: Month _____ Day _____ Year _____

Blood type: _____

Social Security number: _____

Medicare number: _____

Medicaid number: _____

Secondary insurance name: _____

Address: _____

Phone: _____

Policy number: _____

Name known food allergies: _____

Name known drug allergies: _____

Date and reason for all hospitalizations (as an adult):

_____   _____
_____   _____
_____   _____
_____   _____
_____   _____

Past medical problems:

_____
_____
_____
_____
_____
_____

Notify in case of emergency:

Name: _____ Phone: _____

Name: _____ Phone: _____

Medicine Chart

- Update this chart after each doctor visit.

- List both prescribed medications and OTC (over the counter) preparations.

- Draw a red line through any medications stopped, and date it.

Name of Drug Taking	Dosage	Times for Taking	Prescription Number	Date Started

Monthly Meal Planner

Number your recipe books. Write recipe book number in parentheses and recipe name on the line.

Day	Noon	Evening
1 ( )	_____	( ) _____
2 ( )	_____	( ) _____
3 ( )	_____	( ) _____
4 ( )	_____	( ) _____
5 ( )	_____	( ) _____
6 ( )	_____	( ) _____
7 ( )	_____	( ) _____
8 ( )	_____	( ) _____
9 ( )	_____	( ) _____
10 ( )	_____	( ) _____
11 ( )	_____	( ) _____
12 ( )	_____	( ) _____
13 ( )	_____	( ) _____
14 ( )	_____	( ) _____
15 ( )	_____	( ) _____
16 ( )	_____	( ) _____
17 ( )	_____	( ) _____
18 ( )	_____	( ) _____
19 ( )	_____	( ) _____
20 ( )	_____	( ) _____
21 ( )	_____	( ) _____
22 ( )	_____	( ) _____
23 ( )	_____	( ) _____
24 ( )	_____	( ) _____
25 ( )	_____	( ) _____
26 ( )	_____	( ) _____
27 ( )	_____	( ) _____
28 ( )	_____	( ) _____
29 ( )	_____	( ) _____
30 ( )	_____	( ) _____
31 ( )	_____	( ) _____

Nursing Home Checklist

Visit each nursing home on your list at least once, unannounced, and several times if possible. To get the best idea of how a home is run, the following times to visit are suggested: Meals, 4-8 P.M., weekends, and holidays.

	Yes	No
I. Building and Furnishings		
Certificates and licenses on display?	☐	☐
Free of hazards underfoot?	☐	☐
Walls clean, painted?	☐	☐
Towels fresh?	☐	☐
Bedding clean?	☐	☐
Strong body and urine odors?	☐	☐
Attractively decorated?	☐	☐
Barbers and beauticians available?	☐	☐
Near a hospital?	☐	☐
Well-lit halls, bathrooms?	☐	☐
Sturdy chairs?	☐	☐
Handrails in hallways?	☐	☐
Grab bars in bathrooms?	☐	☐
Exits clearly marked?	☐	☐
Exit doors with panic bars inside?	☐	☐
Doors to stairways kept closed?	☐	☐
Written emergency evacuation plan in sight?	☐	☐
Atmosphere welcoming?	☐	☐
Toilets convenient?	☐	☐
Ramps for handicapped?	☐	☐
II. Staff		
Administrator have current state license?	☐	☐
Neat?	☐	☐
Well groomed?	☐	☐
Considerate?	☐	☐
Working with patients?	☐	☐
Clustered at nursing station?	☐	☐
Nowhere in sight?	☐	☐
Speak to patients as adults?	☐	☐
Staff certified?	☐	☐
Physician visits every 30 or 60 days?	☐	☐
Private physician allowed?	☐	☐
Certified dietician on staff?	☐	☐
Extra staff to help feed?	☐	☐
Dentists available regularly?	☐	☐

	Yes	No
Optometrist available regularly?	☐	☐
Social worker available?	☐	☐
Responds quickly to calls?	☐	☐
III. Bedrooms		
Open into hall?	☐	☐
Windows?	☐	☐
Nurse call bell?	☐	☐
Fresh drinking water at each bed?	☐	☐
Comfortable chair?	☐	☐
Reading light?	☐	☐
Clothes closet?	☐	☐
Drawers for personal items?	☐	☐
Free of unpleasant odor?	☐	☐
Privacy for personal needs?	☐	☐
Decorate own rooms?	☐	☐
IV. Food		
Look appetizing?	☐	☐
Fresh fruit served?	☐	☐
Vegetables served?	☐	☐
Food served on regular dishes with silverware?	☐	☐
Food served on paper plates/plastic utensils?	☐	☐
Staff assist those who cannot feed themselves?	☐	☐
Can patients get food they like?	☐	☐
Meals served in attractive dining room?	☐	☐
Are specific diets available?	☐	☐
Variety from meal to meal?	☐	☐
Snacks?	☐	☐
Ample time given for each meal?	☐	☐
V. Services		
Group activities with option to participate?	☐	☐
Individual activities with option to participate?	☐	☐
Outside trips?	☐	☐

	Yes	No
Recreational therapy?	☐	☐
Physical therapy?	☐	☐
Speech therapy?	☐	☐
Religious services offered?	☐	☐
Adequate laundry system?	☐	☐
Resident council?	☐	☐

VI. Finances

	Yes	No
Deposit required?	☐	☐
When patient's private funds are gone, is deposit returned?	☐	☐

	Yes	No
Does home keep patients when they apply for Medicaid (Title 19)?	☐	☐
Patients handle own personal funds?	☐	☐
Patients handle personal belongings?	☐	☐

VII. Patients

	Yes	No
Hair clean and combed?	☐	☐
Clothing clean?	☐	☐
Involved in activities?	☐	☐
Look healthy?	☐	☐
Look listless?	☐	☐
Restraints used?	☐	☐

"One Anothers" of Scripture

1. **LOVE ONE ANOTHER**—John 13:34-35; 15:12-13; Rom. 13:8; 1 Thess. 3:12; 4:9-10; 1 Pet. 1:22; 4:8; 1 John 3:11, 16-18, 22-23; 4:4-7, 11-12, 19-21; 5:2; 2 John 5-6.

2. **ACCEPT ONE ANOTHER**—Rom. 14:1; 15:7.

3. **SERVE ONE ANOTHER**—Mark 10:43-45; Luke 22:26-27; Gal. 5:13; 1 Pet. 4:10-11.

4. **BUILD UP ONE ANOTHER**—Rom. 14:19; 15:2; Eph. 4:15-16, 29; 1 Thess. 5:11.

5. **SEEK ONE ANOTHER'S GOOD**—1 Cor. 10:24; Gal. 6:10; Phil. 2:4.

6. **ENCOURAGE ONE ANOTHER**—1 Thess. 3:2; 4:18; 5:11; Heb. 3:13; 10:25.

7. **CARRY (BEAR) ONE ANOTHER'S BURDENS**—Gal. 6:10; Phil. 2:4.

8. **LIVE IN HARMONY AND UNITY WITH ONE ANOTHER**—Rom. 12:16; 15:5-6.

9. **SUBMIT TO ONE ANOTHER**—1 Cor. 16:15-16; Eph. 5:21.

10. **HAVE CONCERN FOR ONE ANOTHER**—1 Cor. 12:25; Phil. 2:20.

11. **BE PATIENT WITH ONE ANOTHER**—Eph. 4:2; Col. 3:13.

12. **FORGIVE ONE ANOTHER**—Matt. 6:14-15; 18:21-35; Mark 11:25; Luke 17:3-4; Eph. 4:32; Col. 3:13.

13. **BE AT PEACE WITH ONE ANOTHER**—Mark 9:50; Rom. 12:18; 14:19; 1 Thess. 5:13; 2 Tim. 2:23; Heb. 12:14.

14. **BE KIND TO ONE ANOTHER**—Eph. 4:32.

15. **DO NOT LIE TO ONE ANOTHER**—Eph. 4:25; Col. 3:9.

16. **DO NOT GRUMBLE AGAINST ONE ANOTHER**—Phil. 2:14; James 5:9.

17. **PRAY FOR ONE ANOTHER**—James 5:16.

18. **DO NOT PROVOKE ONE ANOTHER**—Gal. 5:26.

Prayer Requests

1. In the center column, write the prayer request you are bringing to God. Be specific.

2. In the left column, write the date you begin praying for the request.

3. In the right column, write the date when God answers.

Date of Request	Prayer Request	Date of Answer

BIBLIOGRAPHY

Anderson-Ellis, Eugenia, and Marsha Dryan. *Aging Parents and You*. New York: Master Media, 1988.

Armstrong, Mary Vaughn. *Caregiving for Your Loved Ones*. Elgin, Ill.: David C. Cook Publishing Co., 1990.

Bathauer, Ruth M. *Parent Care*. Ventura, Calif.: Regal Books, 1990.

Cadmus, Robert R. *Caring for Your Aging Parents: A Concerned, Complete Guide for Children of the Elderly*. Old Tappan, N.J.: Prentice-Hall, 1984.

Clifford, Denis. *The Power of Attorney Book*. Berkeley, Calif.: Nolo Press, 1986.

———. *The Simple Will Book*. Berkeley, Calif.: Nolo Press, 1986.

Colen, B. D. *The Essential Guide to a Living Will*. New York: Prentice Hall Press, 1991.

Crichton, Jean. *The Age Care Sourcebook: A Resource Guide for the Aging and Their Families*. New York: Simon and Schuster, 1987.

Deane, Barbara. *Caring for Your Aging Parents*. Colorado Springs: NavPress, 1989.

Dillow, Linda. *Priority Planner*. Nashville: Thomas Nelson, 1986.

DuFresne, Florine. *Home Care: An Alternative to the Nursing Home*. Elgin, Ill.: Brethren Press, 1985.

Edinberg, Mark A. *Talking with Your Aging Parents*. Boston: Shambhala Publications, 1987.

Foehner, Charlotte, and Carol Cozart. *The Widow's Handbook*. Golden, Colo.: Fulcrum, 1988.

Gibson, Dennis, and Ruth Gibson. *The Sandwich Years*. Grand Rapids: Baker Book House, 1991.

Gillies, John. *Care Giving*. Wheaton, Ill.: Harold Shaw Publishers, 1988.

Green, Tracy, and Todd Temple. *52 Ways to Show Aging Parents You Care*. Nashville: Thomas Nelson Publishers, 1992.

Horne, Jo. *A Survival Guide for Family Caregivers*. Minneapolis: CompCare Publishers, 1991.

———. *The Nursing Home Handbook*. Glenview, Ill.: Scott, Foresman and Co., 1989.

Jacobsen, Jamia Jasper, ed. *Help! I'm Parenting My Parents*. Indianapolis: Benchmark Press, 1988.

Jamison, Bonnie. *Take Me Home*. Wheaton, Ill.: Tyndale House Publishers, 1986.

Jarvik, Lissy, and Gary Small. *Parentcare*. New York: Bantam Books, 1990.

Jehle, Faustin F. *The Complete and Easy Guide to Social Security and Medicare*. 1989 ed. Madison, Conn.: Fraser Publishing Co., 1989.

Johnson, Richard P. *Aging Parents: How to Understand and Help Them*. Liguori, Mo.: Liguori Publications, 1987.

Levin, Nora Jean. *How to Care for Your Parents*. Friday Harbor, Wash.: Storm King Press, 1990.

Levy, Michael T. *Parenting Mom and Dad*. New York: Prentice Hall Press, 1991.

McLean, Helene. *Caring for Your Parents: A Sourcebook of Options and Solutions for Both Generations*. Garden City, N.Y.: Doubleday, 1987.

Mace, Nancy L. and Peter V. Rabins. *The 36-Hour Day—A Family Guide to Caring for Persons with Alzheimer's Disease, Related Dementing Illnesses, and Memory Loss in Later Life*. Baltimore: John Hopkins, 1991.

Mall, E. Jane. *Caregiving*. New York: Ballantine Books, 1990.

———. *How to Care for Your Elderly Mother and Stay Sane*. New York: Ballantine Books, 1990.

Matthew, Joseph. *Elder Care—Choosing and Financing Long-Term Care*. Berkeley, Calif.: Nolo Press, 1991.

Moskowitz, Francine, and Robert Moskowitz. *Parenting Your Aging Parents*. Woodland Hills, Calif.: Key Publications, 1991.

Neidrick, Darla J. *Caring for Your Own*. New York: John Wiley and Sons, 1988.

Riekse, Dr. Robert J., and Dr. Henry Holstege. *The Christian Guide to Parent Care*. Wheaton, Ill.: Tyndale House Publishers, 1992.

Rob, Caroline. *The Caregiver's Guide: Helping Elderly Relatives Cope with Health and Safety Problems*. Boston: Houghton Mifflin Co., 1991.

Rushford, Patricia H. *The Help, Hope, and Cope Book for People with Aging Parents*. Old Tappan, N.J.: Fleming H. Revell Co., 1985.

Sargent, Jean Vieth. *An Easier Way—Handbook for the Elderly and Handicapped*. New York: Walker and Co., 1981.

Shelley, Florence D., and Jane Otten. *When Your Parents Grow Old*. New York: Harper and Row, 1988.

Silver, Don. *A Parent's Guide to Wills and Trusts*. Los Angeles: Adams-Hall Publishing, 1992.

Silverstone, Barbara, and Helen Hyman. *You and Your Aging Parent*. New York: Pantheon Books, 1989.

Soled, Alex J. *The Essential Guide to Wills, Estates, Trusts, and Death Taxes*. Glenview, Ill.: Scott, Foresman, and Co., 1988.

Stafford, Tim. *As Our Years Increase*. Grand Rapids: Zondervan Publishing House, 1989.

Thompson, M. Keith. *Caring for an Elderly Relative*. New York: Prentice Hall Press, 1986.

Thornton, Howard A., M.D. *A Medical Handbook for Seniors and Their Families*. Dover, Mass.: Auburn House Publishing Co., 1989.